THE ULTIMATE UK NINJA Speedi

COOKBOOK FOR BEGINNER

1000 Days Quick and Delicious Recipes with Easy-to-Follow Guide to Speedi Meals, Bake, Roast and Slow Cook for Smart People

Matilda Law

Copyright © 2023 By Matilda Law All rights reserved.

No part of this book may be reproduced, transmitted, or distributed in any form or by any means without permission in writing from the publisher except in the case of brief quotations embodied in critical articles or reviews.

Legal & Disclaimer

The content and information in this book is consistent and truthful, and it has been provided for informational, educational and business purposes only.

The illustrations in the book are from the website shutterstock.com, depositphoto.com and freepik.com and have been authorized.

The content and information contained in this book has been compiled from reliable sources, which are accurate based on the knowledge, belief, expertise and information of the Author. The author cannot be held liable for any omissions and/or errors.

Table of Content

Introduction ··· 1

CHAPTER 1 BREAKFAST ··· 2

Pitta Pepperoni Pizza ································ 3
Spinach and Egg Cups ······························· 3
Sweetcorn Sausage Frittata ······················· 4
Cinnamon Apple Nut Muffins ··················· 4
Simple Vanilla Donuts ································ 5
Broccoli and Chicken Quiche ···················· 5
Kale and Potato Nuggets ··························· 6
Tasty Ricotta Toasts ·································· 6
Ham and Tomato Omelette ······················· 7
Mozzarella Pitta Pizza ································ 7
Healthy Egg Veggie Frittata ······················ 8
Ham and Egg Toast Cups ··························· 8
Quick Sausage Pizza ··································· 9
Mini Tomato and Gouda Quiche ··············· 9
Tofu Scramble Omelette ·························· 10
Delish Mushroom Frittata ························ 10

Chapter 2 FISH AND SEAFOOD ·· 11

Creamy Breaded Prawn ··························· 12
Garlic Scallops ··· 12
Tasty Cod Sticks ······································ 13
Tuna Patty Sliders ··································· 13
Panko Salmon Patties ····························· 14
Bacon-Wrapped Prawn ···························· 14
Easy Roasted Salmon ······························· 15
Scallops with Capers Sauce ····················· 15
Mediterranean Cod and Veggies ············ 16
Salmon and Veggies Ratatouille ············· 16
Spicy Orange Prawn ································ 17
Spiced Catfish with Spaghetti ················· 17
Savory Tuna Cakes ·································· 18
Salmon Vegetables Chowder ·················· 18
Rice Noodles with Broccoli and Scallop ··· 19
Prawn and Polenta with Tomato ············ 19
Honey Glazed Salmon with Sweet Potato Rice ··· 20

Chapter 3 VEGETABLES ·· 21

Sweet Potato Chips ································· 22
Italian Aubergine Slices ··························· 22
Cheese Stuffed Tomatoes ······················· 23
Crispy Cornmeal Okra ····························· 23
Blistered Shishito Peppers ······················ 24
Braised Sweet and Sour Red Cabbage ··· 24
French Green Beans with Shallot ··········· 25
Roasted Potatoes and Asparagus ··········· 25
Vegetable Ratatouille ······························ 26
Brussels Sprouts ······································ 26
Sweet Potatoes with Carrot ···················· 27
Garlic Root Vegetable Hash ···················· 27
Honey-Glazed Parsnips, Carrots and Fennel ··· 28
Curried Winter Squash ···························· 28
Rosemary White Beans with Onion ······· 29
Buttered Sweetcorn on the Cob ············· 29

Chapter 4 LAMB, BEEF AND PORK … 30

Classic Sweet and Sour Pork and Pineapple … 31	Chili Pork with Vegetable Quinoa … 35
Citrus Roasted Pork … 31	Cheesy Sausage Balls and Bulgur Wheat … 36
Gourmet Meatloaf … 32	Cheddar Bacon Burst with Spinach … 36
Sweet and Spicy Pepper Beef Jerky … 32	Beef Meatballs and Tomato Meal … 37
Beef Roast with Mushroom and Carrot … 33	Corned Beef … 37
Tasty Beef Roast … 33	Italian Lamb Chops with Avocado Mayo … 38
Roasted Lamb Leg … 34	Spiced Lamb Steaks and Snap Pea Rice … 38
Mustard Lamb Ribs … 34	Chinese Lamb … 39
Japanese Tamari Pork … 35	

Chapter 5 POULTRY … 40

Crispy Chicken Drumsticks … 41	Crisp Chicken and Creamy Polenta … 46
Air Fried Chicken Tenders … 41	Broccoli and Chicken … 47
Cheesy Chicken Stuffed Mushrooms … 42	Yummy Stuffed Chicken Breast with Fettuccine … 47
Chicken Meatballs … 42	Curry Chicken with Dried Cranberry … 48
Chicken Manchurian … 43	Chicken Meatballs with Scallion … 48
Little Bay Yellow Curry … 43	Traditional Chicken Provençal … 49
Cheesy Chicken Tacos … 44	Chicken Pomegranate Stew … 49
Easy Tandoori Chicken … 45	Chicken Tenders with Broccoli Quinoa Meal … 50
Sausage Stuffed Chicken and Corn Rice … 46	

Chapter 6 SNACK AND DESSERT … 51

Spicy Kale Crisps … 52	Chocolate Cherry Turnovers … 56
Fluffy Orange Cake … 52	Sweet and Spicy Carrot Sticks … 57
Tasty Chicken Wings … 53	Potato and Bacon Nuggets … 57
Strawberries … 53	Bacon Filled Poppers … 58
Crispy Spiced Chickpeas … 54	Root Veggie Crisps with Herb Salt … 58
Crispy Bacon-Wrapped Dates … 54	Tropical Fruit Sticks … 59
Raspberry Wontons … 55	Fruity Crumble … 59
Walnut Chocolate Cake … 55	Doughnuts Pudding … 60
Frosting Cupcakes … 56	

APPENDIX 1: NINJA SPEEDI TIMETABLE … 61
APPENDIX 2: RECIPES INDEX … 66

INTRODUCTION

As I stood in my kitchen, staring at the Ninja Speedi Rapid Cooker on my worktop, I couldn't help but think about how this little appliance had changed my life. It had quickly become my go-to tool for preparing quick, healthy meals for myself and my family.

I had always struggled with finding the time and energy to cook, especially after a long day at work. I found myself relying on takeout and processed foods more often than I'd like to admit. But the Ninja Speedi Rapid Cooker had changed all of that. It was fast, versatile, and easy to use, making it the perfect solution for busy weeknights.

As I experimented with different recipes and cooking methods, I realized that this little appliance had so much potential. It could steam, air fry, grill, bake, and even dehydrate! The possibilities were endless.

That's when the idea for this cookbook was born. I wanted to share my love for the Ninja Speedi Rapid Cooker with others and show them just how versatile and convenient this appliance could be. I spent countless hours in the kitchen, testing and perfecting recipes, until I had a collection that I was truly proud of.

In this cookbook, you'll find a variety of recipes that can be prepared quickly and easily using the Ninja Speedi Rapid Cooker. From starters and snacks to main dishes and desserts, there's something for everyone. You'll find healthy, nutritious meals that are perfect for busy weeknights, as well as indulgent treats that are perfect for special occasions.

I hope that this cookbook will inspire you to explore the possibilities of the Ninja Speedi Rapid Cooker and discover just how much it can do. Whether you're a seasoned cook or a beginner, this cookbook has something for everyone. So, grab your apron, fire up your Ninja Speedi Rapid Cooker, and let's get cooking!

Overview of the Ninja Speedi Rapid Cooker and Air Fryer

The Ninja Speedi Rapid Cooker and Air Fryer is a versatile kitchen appliance that offers a variety of cooking functions, allowing you to prepare a wide range of meals with ease. It uses a combination of superheated steam and air to cook your food quickly and evenly, while the air frying function gives your food a crispy texture without the need for excess oil.

This appliance is designed with convenience in mind, featuring a user-friendly control panel with clearly labeled cooking functions and a digital timer for precise cooking. The Smart Switch allows you to easily switch between Rapid Cooker mode and Air Fry/Hob cooking modes, unlocking a range of cooking functions to suit different types of food and cooking situations.

Whether you want to cook a quick and healthy meal for yourself or prepare a delicious feast for the whole family, the Ninja Speedi Rapid Cooker and Air Fryer has got you covered. With its versatile cooking functions and easy-to-use features, this appliance is sure to become a go-to tool in your kitchen.

What will you get from this cookbook?

The Ninja Speedi Cookbook includes a wide range of recipe categories to suit every taste and dietary need. Whether you're looking for keto-friendly recipes, gluten-free options, or vegetarian meals, you'll find plenty of delicious options to choose from.

So if you're ready to take your cooking game to the next level, look no further than the Ninja Speedi Cookbook. With its delicious recipes, comprehensive instructions, and beautiful design, it's the ultimate guide to making the most of your Ninja Speedi Rapid Cooker and Air Fryer.

CHAPTER 1
BREAKFAST

Pitta Pepperoni Pizza

Prep: 10 minutes, Total Cook Time: 21 minutes, Steam: approx. 15 minutes, Cook: 6 minutes, Serves: 4

INGREDIENTS:

- 250 ml water, for steaming
- cooking spray
- 1 pitta bread
- 25 g grated mozzarella cheese
- 7 slices pepperoni
- 25 g sausage
- 1 tbsp. yellow onion, thinly sliced
- 1 tbsp. tomato puree
- 1 drizzle extra-virgin olive oil
- ½ tsp. fresh garlic, minced

DIRECTIONS:

1. Pour 250 ml water into the pot. Push in the legs on the Cook & Crisp tray, then place the tray in the bottom position in the pot. Spray Multi-Purpose Tin or 20cm cake tin with cooking spray.
2. Spread tomato puree on the pitta bread and add sausages, pepperoni, onions, garlic and cheese.
3. Drizzle with olive oil and transfer the pitta bread to the prepared tin, then place the tin on the tray.
4. Close the lid and flip the SmartSwitch to RAPID COOKER. Select STEAM BAKE, set temperature to 180°C, and set time to 6 minutes. Press START/STOP to begin cooking (the unit will steam for approx. 15 minutes, before countdown time begins).
5. Dish out to serve warm.

Spinach and Egg Cups

Prep: 15 minutes, Total Cook Time: 41 minutes, Steam: approx. 20 minutes, Cook: 21 minutes, Serves: 4

INGREDIENTS:

- 250 ml water, for steaming
- 15 g unsalted butter, melted
- 450 g fresh baby spinach
- 4 eggs
- 200 g ham, sliced
- 20 ml milk
- 15 ml olive oil
- Salt and black pepper, to taste

DIRECTIONS:

1. Pour 250 ml water into the pot. Push in the legs on the Cook & Crisp tray, then place the tray in the bottom position in the pot. Grease 4 ramekins with butter.
2. Heat olive oil in a frying pan and add spinach.
3. Sauté for about 3 minutes and drain the liquid completely from the spinach.
4. Divide the spinach equally into the prepared ramekins and add ham slices.
5. Crack 1 egg over ham in each ramekin and pour milk evenly over eggs.
6. Season with salt and black pepper and transfer the ramekins on the tray.
7. Close the lid and flip the SmartSwitch to RAPID COOKER. Select STEAM BAKE, set temperature to 180°C, and set time to 18 minutes. Press START/STOP to begin cooking (the unit will steam for approx. 20 minutes, before countdown time begins).
8. Serve warm.

Sweetcorn Sausage Frittata

Prep: 15 minutes, Total Cook Time: 22 minutes, Steam: approx. 10 minutes, Cook: 12 minutes, Serves: 2

INGREDIENTS:

- 250 ml water, for steaming
- cooking spray
- 75 g chorizo sausage, sliced
- 75 g frozen sweetcorn
- 1 large potato, boiled, peeled and cubed
- 3 large eggs
- 30 g feta cheese, crumbled
- 15 ml olive oil
- Salt and black pepper, to taste

DIRECTIONS:

1. Pour 250 ml water into the pot. Push in the legs on the Cook & Crisp tray, then place the tray in the bottom position in the pot. Spray Multi-Purpose Tin or 20cm cake tin with cooking spray.
2. Whisk together eggs with salt and black pepper in a bowl.
3. Heat olive oil in a skillet over medium heat, add sausage, sweetcorn and potato. Sauté for 5 minutes. Then transfer into the tin and stir in the whisked eggs. Place on the tray and top with cheese.
4. Close the lid and flip the SmartSwitch to RAPID COOKER. Select STEAM BAKE, set temperature to 180°C, and set time to 7 minutes. Press START/STOP to begin cooking (the unit will steam for approx. 10 minutes, before countdown time begins).
5. When cooking is complete, dish out and serve hot.

Cinnamon Apple Nut Muffins

Prep: 10 minutes, Total Cook Time: 10 minutes, Serves: 8 muffins

INGREDIENTS:

- 120 g flour
- 75 g caster sugar
- 180 g unsweetened applesauce
- 30 g chopped walnuts
- 50 g diced apple
- 1 tsp. baking powder
- ¼ tsp. bicarbonate of soda
- ¼ tsp. salt
- 1 tsp. cinnamon
- ¼ tsp. ground ginger
- ¼ tsp. ground nutmeg
- 1 egg
- 40 ml pancake syrup
- 40 g melted butter
- ½ tsp. vanilla extract

DIRECTIONS:

1. Push in the legs on the Cook & Crisp tray, then place the tray in the bottom of the pot.
2. In a large bowl, stir together the flour, baking powder, bicarbonate of soda, caster sugar, salt, cinnamon, ginger, and nutmeg.
3. In a small bowl, beat the egg until frothy. Place syrup, butter, applesauce, and vanilla and combine well.
4. Pour the egg mixture into dry ingredients and stir just until moistened.
5. Carefully stir in nuts and diced apple.
6. Divide the batter evenly among 8 parchment-paper-lined muffin cups.
7. Close the lid and flip the SmartSwitch to AIR FRY/HOB. Select BAKE & ROAST, set temperature to 165°C, and set time to 15 minutes (unit will need to preheat for 5 minutes, so set an external timer if desired). Press START/STOP to begin cooking.
8. When the unit is preheated and the time reaches 10 minutes, put 4 muffin cups on the tray. Close the lid to begin cooking.
9. Repeat with remaining 4 muffins or until toothpick inserted in centre comes out clean.
10. When cooking is complete, serve warm.

Simple Vanilla Donuts

Prep: 10 minutes, Total Cook Time: 30 minutes, Steam: approx. 20 minutes, Cook: 10 minutes, Serves: 3

INGREDIENTS:

- 250 ml water, for steaming
- cooking spray
- 200 g plain flour
- 2 tsps. baking powder
- 1 egg
- 15 g butter, softened
- 120 ml milk
- Pinch of salt
- 150 g caster sugar
- 2 tsps. vanilla extract
- 25 g icing sugar

DIRECTIONS:

1. Pour 250 ml water into the pot. Push in the legs on the Cook & Crisp tray, then place the tray in the bottom position in the pot. Spray Multi-Purpose Tin or 20cm cake tin with cooking spray.
2. Sift together flour, baking powder and salt in a large bowl.
3. Add caster sugar and egg and mix well.
4. Stir in the butter, milk and vanilla extract and mix until a dough is formed.
5. Refrigerate the dough for at least 1 hour and roll the dough into 1-cm thickness onto a floured surface.
6. Cut into donuts with a donut cutter and arrange the donuts on the tin(You may need cook in two batches). Place the tin on the tray.
7. Close the lid and flip the SmartSwitch to RAPID COOKER. Select STEAM BAKE, set temperature to 190°C, and set time to 10 minutes. Press START/STOP to begin cooking (the unit will steam for approx. 20 minutes, before countdown time begins), until golden.
8. Sprinkle the icing sugar over the donuts and serve warm.

Broccoli and Chicken Quiche

Prep: 15 minutes, Total Cook Time: 27 minutes, Steam: approx. 15 minutes, Cook: 12 minutes, Serves: 4

INGREDIENTS:

- 250 ml water, for steaming
- 1 frozen ready-made shortcrust pastry
- 1 egg
- 50 g cheddar cheese, grated
- 60 g boiled broccoli, chopped
- 60 g cooked chicken, chopped
- 7 ml olive oil
- 45 ml single cream
- Salt and black pepper, to taste

DIRECTIONS:

1. Pour 250 ml water into the pot. Push in the legs on the Cook & Crisp tray, then place the tray in the bottom position in the pot. Spray 2 small pie pans with cooking spray.
2. Whisk egg with single cream, cheese, salt and black pepper in a bowl.
3. Cut 2 (12.5-cm) rounds from the shortcrust crust and arrange in each pie pan.
4. Press in the bottom and sides gently and pour the egg mixture over pie crust.
5. Top evenly with chicken and broccoli and place the pie pans on the tray.
6. Close the lid and flip the SmartSwitch to RAPID COOKER. Select STEAM BAKE, set temperature to 200°C, and set time to 12 minutes. Press START/STOP to begin cooking (the unit will steam for approx. 15 minutes, before countdown time begins).
7. Dish out to serve hot.

Kale and Potato Nuggets

Prep: 10 minutes, Total Cook Time: 20 minutes, Serves: 4

INGREDIENTS:

- Cooking spray
- 5 ml extra virgin olive oil
- 300 g kale, rinsed and chopped
- 400 g potatoes, boiled and mashed
- 30 ml milk
- 1 clove garlic, minced
- Salt and ground black pepper, to taste

DIRECTIONS:

1. Push in the legs on the Cook & Crisp tray, then place the tray in the bottom of the pot. Spray the tray with cooking spray.
2. In a skillet, sauté the garlic over medium heat in the olive oil, until it turns golden brown. Sauté with the kale for an additional 3 minutes and remove from the heat.
3. Combine the mashed potatoes, kale and garlic in a bowl. Pour in the milk and sprinkle with salt and pepper.
4. Form the mixture into nuggets and spritz with cooking spray.
5. Close the lid and flip the SmartSwitch to AIR FRY/HOB. Select AIRFRY, set temperature to 200°C, and set time to 22 minutes (unit will need to preheat for 5 minutes, so set an external timer if desired). Press START/STOP to begin cooking.
6. When the unit is preheated and the time reaches 17 minutes, place the nuggets on the tray. Close the lid to begin cooking.
7. After 8 minutes, open the lid and toss the nuggets with silicone-tipped tongs to ensure even cooking. Close the lid to continue cooking.
8. When cooking is complete, serve the nuggets hot.

Tasty Ricotta Toasts

Prep Time: 10 minutes, Cook Time: 5 minutes, Serves: 4

INGREDIENTS:

- cooking spray
- 4 bread slices
- 225 g ricotta cheese
- 115 g smoked salmon
- 1 shallot, sliced
- 40 g rocket
- 1 garlic clove, minced
- 1 tsp. lemon zest
- ¼ tsp. freshly ground black pepper

DIRECTIONS:

1. Push in the legs on the Cook & Crisp tray, then place the tray in the bottom of the pot. Spray the tray with cooking spray.
2. Close the lid and flip the SmartSwitch to AIR FRY/HOB. Select BAKE & ROAST, set temperature to 180°C, and set time to 10 minutes (unit will need to preheat for 5 minutes, so set an external timer if desired). Press START/STOP to begin cooking.
3. When the unit is preheated and the time reaches 5 minutes, place the bread slices on the tray. Close the lid to begin cooking.
4. Put garlic, ricotta cheese and lemon zest in a food processor and pulse until smooth.
5. Spread this mixture over each bread slice and top with salmon, rocket and shallot.
6. Sprinkle with black pepper and serve warm.

Ham and Tomato Omelette

Prep: 10 minutes, Total Cook Time: 37 minutes, Steam: approx. 15 minutes, Cook: 22 minutes, Serves: 2

INGREDIENTS:

- 250 ml water, for steaming
- cooking spray
- 4 small tomatoes, chopped
- 4 eggs
- 2 ham slices
- 1 onion, chopped
- 2 tbsp. cheddar cheese
- Salt and black pepper, to taste

DIRECTIONS:

1. Pour 250 ml water into the pot. Push in the legs on the Cook & Crisp tray, then place the tray in the bottom position in the pot. Spray Multi-Purpose Tin or 20cm cake tin with cooking spray.
2. Heat a nonstick skillet over medium heat and add onion and ham. Stir fry for about 5 minutes.
3. Place the tomatoes in the tin, then transfer the tin on the tray.
4. Close the lid and flip the SmartSwitch to RAPID COOKER. Select STEAM BAKE, set temperature to 180°C, and set time to 17 minutes. Press START/STOP to begin cooking (the unit will steam for approx. 15 minutes, before countdown time begins).
5. With 10 minutes remaining, open the lid. Transfer the onion mixture into the pan. Whisk together eggs, cheddar cheese, salt and black pepper in a bowl and pour in the tin. Close the lid to continue cooking.
6. Dish out and serve warm.

Mozzarella Pitta Pizza

Prep: 10 minutes, Total Cook Time: 12 minutes, Steam: approx. 4 minutes, Cook: 8 minutes, Serves: 1

INGREDIENTS:

- 125 ml water, for steaming
- 15 ml tomato sauce
- 1 pitta bread
- 6 pepperoni slices
- 25 g grated Mozzarella cheese
- ¼ tsp. garlic powder
- ¼ tsp. dried oregano

DIRECTIONS:

1. Pour 125 ml water into the pot. Push in the legs on the Cook & Crisp tray, then place the tray in the bottom position in the pot.
2. Spread the tomato sauce on top of the pitta bread. Put the pepperoni slices over the sauce, followed by the Mozzarella cheese.
3. Season with garlic powder and oregano. Transfer the pitta pizza to the tray.
4. Close the lid and flip the SmartSwitch to RAPID COOKER. Select STEAM AIR FRY, set temperature to 180°C, and set time to 8 minutes. Press START/STOP to begin cooking (the unit will steam for approx. 4 minutes, before countdown time begins).
5. When cooking is complete, use tongs to remove the pizza from the tray and serve hot.

Healthy Egg Veggie Frittata

Prep: 10 minutes, Total Cook Time: 35 minutes, Steam: approx. 20 minutes, Cook: 15 minutes, Serves: 2

INGREDIENTS:

- 250 ml water, for steaming
- 4 eggs
- 120 ml milk
- 2 spring onions, chopped
- 25 g baby Bella mushrooms, chopped
- 25 g spinach, chopped
- 15 g butter
- ½ tsp. Salt
- ½ tsp. black pepper
- Dash of hot sauce

DIRECTIONS:

1. Pour 250 ml water into the pot. Push in the legs on the Cook & Crisp tray, then place the tray in the bottom position in the pot. Grease a 15x8 cm square pan with butter.
2. Whisk eggs with milk in a large bowl and stir in spring onions, mushrooms and spinach.
3. Sprinkle with salt, black pepper and hot sauce and pour this mixture into the prepared pan. Then place the pan on the tray.
4. Close the lid and flip the SmartSwitch to RAPID COOKER. Select STEAM BAKE, set temperature to 180°C, and set time to 15 minutes. Press START/STOP to begin cooking (the unit will steam for approx. 20 minutes, before countdown time begins).
5. Dish out in a platter and serve warm.

Ham and Egg Toast Cups

Prep Time: 5 minutes, Cook Time: 6 minutes, Serves: 2

INGREDIENTS:

- 2 eggs
- 2 slices of ham
- 30 g butter, melted
- Cheddar cheese, for topping
- Salt, to taste
- Black pepper, to taste

DIRECTIONS:

1. Push in the legs on the Cook & Crisp tray, then place the tray in the bottom of the pot. Grease both ramekins with melted butter.
2. Place each ham slice in the greased ramekins and crack each egg over ham slices.
3. Sprinkle with salt, black pepper and cheddar cheese.
4. Close the lid and flip the SmartSwitch to AIR FRY/HOB. Select BAKE & ROAST, set temperature to 205°C, and set time to 11 minutes (unit will need to preheat for 5 minutes, so set an external timer if desired). Press START/STOP to begin cooking.
5. When the unit is preheated and the time reaches 6 minutes, place the ramekins on the tray. Close the lid to begin cooking.
6. When cooking is complete, remove the ramekins from tray. Serve hot.

Quick Sausage Pizza

Prep: 10 minutes, Total Cook Time: 12 minutes, Steam: approx. 4 minutes, Cook: 8 minutes, Serves: 4

INGREDIENTS:

- 250 ml water, for steaming
- 30 ml tomato ketchup
- 80 g sausage
- 225 g Mozzarella cheese
- 1 pitta bread
- 1 tsp. garlic powder
- 15 ml olive oil

DIRECTIONS:

1. Pour 250 ml water into the pot. Push in the legs on the Cook & Crisp tray, then place the tray in the bottom position in the pot.
2. Spread the tomato ketchup over the pitta bread.
3. Top with the sausage and cheese. Sprinkle with the garlic powder and olive oil. Place the pizza on the tray.
4. Close the lid and flip the SmartSwitch to RAPID COOKER. Select STEAM AIR FRY, set temperature to 180°C, and set time to 8 minutes. Press START/STOP to begin cooking (the unit will steam for approx. 4 minutes, before countdown time begins).
5. When cooking is complete, remove the pizza from the tray and serve warm.

Mini Tomato and Gouda Quiche

Prep: 15 minutes, Total Cook Time: 35 minutes, Steam: approx. 20 minutes, Cook: 15 minutes, Serves: 2

INGREDIENTS:

- 250 ml water, for steaming
- cooking spray
- 4 eggs
- 25 g onion, chopped
- 75 g tomatoes, chopped
- 120 ml milk
- 100 g Gouda cheese, shredded
- Salt, to taste

DIRECTIONS:

1. Pour 250 ml water into the pot. Push in the legs on the Cook & Crisp tray, then place the tray in the bottom position in the pot. Spray a large ramekin with cooking spray.
2. Mix together all the ingredients in the ramekin and transfer on the tray.
3. Close the lid and flip the SmartSwitch to RAPID COOKER. Select STEAM BAKE, set temperature to 165°C, and set time to 15 minutes. Press START/STOP to begin cooking (the unit will steam for approx. 20 minutes, before countdown time begins).
4. Dish out to serve hot.

Tofu Scramble Omelette

Prep: 10 minutes, Total Cook Time: 40 minutes, Steam: approx. 20 minutes, Cook: 20 minutes, Serves: 2

INGREDIENTS:

- 250 ml water, for steaming
- cooking spray
- ¼ of onion, chopped
- 340 g silken tofu, pressed and sliced
- 3 eggs, beaten
- 1 tbsp. chives, chopped
- 1 garlic clove, minced
- 10 ml olive oil
- Salt and black pepper, to taste

DIRECTIONS:

1. Pour 250 ml water into the pot. Push in the legs on the Cook & Crisp tray, then place the tray in the bottom position in the pot. Spray Multi-Purpose Tin or 20cm cake tin with cooking spray.
2. Add onion and garlic to the greased tin. Place the tin on the tray.
3. Close the lid and flip the SmartSwitch to RAPID COOKER. Select STEAM BAKE, set temperature to 180°C, and set time to 20 minutes. Press START/STOP to begin cooking (the unit will steam for approx. 20 minutes, before countdown time begins).
4. With 16 minutes remaining, open the lid. Add tofu, mushrooms and chives and season with salt and black pepper. Beat the eggs and pour over the tofu mixture. Close the lid to continue cooking, poking the eggs twice in between.
5. Dish out and serve warm.

Delish Mushroom Frittata

Prep: 15 minutes, Total Cook Time: 35 minutes, Steam: approx. 20 minutes, Cook: 15 minutes, Serves: 2

INGREDIENTS:

- 250 ml water, for steaming
- cooking spray
- ½ red onion, sliced thinly
- 300 g button mushrooms, sliced thinly
- 3 eggs
- 30 g feta cheese, crumbled
- 15 ml olive oil
- Salt, to taste

DIRECTIONS:

1. Pour 250 ml water into the pot. Push in the legs on the Cook & Crisp tray, then place the tray in the bottom position in the pot. Spray a 15cm ramekin with cooking spray.
2. Heat olive oil on medium heat in a skillet and add onion and mushrooms.
3. Sauté for about 5 minutes and dish out the mushroom mixture in a bowl.
4. Whisk together eggs and salt in a small bowl and transfer into prepared ramekin.
5. Place the mushroom mixture over the eggs and top with feta cheese.
6. Arrange the ramekin on the tray.
7. Close the lid and flip the SmartSwitch to RAPID COOKER. Select STEAM BAKE, set temperature to 180°C, and set time to 10 minutes. Press START/STOP to begin cooking (the unit will steam for approx. 20 minutes, before countdown time begins).
8. Dish out and serve hot.

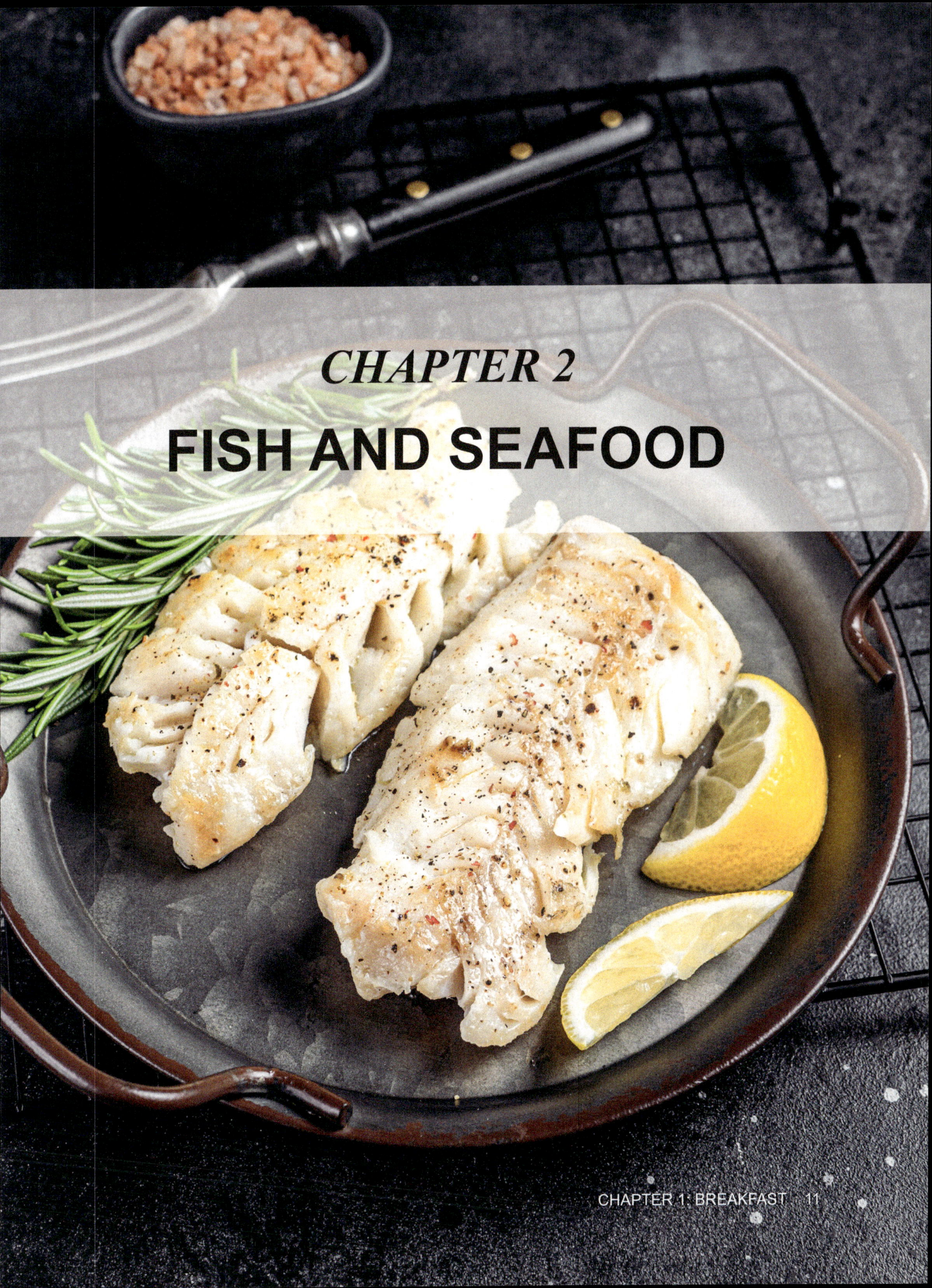

CHAPTER 2
FISH AND SEAFOOD

Creamy Breaded Prawn

Prep: 15 minutes, Total Cook Time: 18 minutes, Steam: approx. 8 minutes, Cook: 10 minutes, Serves: 3

INGREDIENTS:

- 125 ml water, for steaming
- 30 g plain flour
- 80 g panko breadcrumbs
- 450 g prawn, peeled and deveined
- 120 ml mayonnaise
- 60 ml sweet chili sauce
- 1 tbsp. Sriracha sauce

DIRECTIONS:

1. Pour 125 ml water into the pot. Push in the legs on the Cook & Crisp tray, then place the tray in the bottom position in the pot.
2. Place flour in a shallow bowl and mix the mayonnaise, chili sauce, and Sriracha sauce in another bowl.
3. Place the breadcrumbs in a third bowl.
4. Coat each prawn with the flour, dip into mayonnaise mixture and finally, dredge in the breadcrumbs.
5. Arrange half of the coated prawns on the tray.
6. Close the lid and flip the SmartSwitch to RAPID COOKER. Select STEAM AIR FRY, set temperature to 220°C, and set time to 5 minutes. Press START/STOP to begin cooking (the unit will steam for approx. 4 minutes, before countdown time begins).
7. Dish out the prawns onto serving plates.
8. Repeat with the remaining prawns and serve hot.

Garlic Scallops

Prep: 10 minutes, Total Cook Time: 13 minutes, Serves: 4

INGREDIENTS:

- Cooking spray
- 450 g small scallops, patted dry
- 10 ml olive oil
- 1 packet dry zesty Italian dressing mix
- 1 tsp. minced garlic

DIRECTIONS:

1. Push in the legs on the Cook & Crisp tray, then place the tray in the bottom of the pot. Spray the tray with cooking spray.
2. In a large zip-top plastic bag, mix the olive oil, Italian dressing mix, and garlic.
3. Place the scallops, seal the zip-top bag, and coat the scallops evenly in the seasoning mixture.
4. Close the lid and flip the SmartSwitch to AIR FRY/HOB. Select AIRFRY, set temperature to 200°C, and set time to 18 minutes (unit will need to preheat for 5 minutes, so set an external timer if desired). Press START/STOP to begin cooking.
5. When the unit is preheated and the time reaches 13 minutes, place the scallops on the tray. Close the lid to begin cooking.
6. After 7 minutes, open the lid and toss the scallops with silicone-tipped tongs to ensure even cooking. Close the lid to continue cooking, until the scallops reach an internal temperature of 50ºC.
7. Serve immediately.

Tasty Cod Sticks

Prep Time: 20 minutes, Cook Time: 8 minutes, Serves: 2

INGREDIENTS:

- cooking spray
- 3 (110 g each) skinless cod fillets, cut into rectangular pieces
- 75 g plain flour
- 4 eggs
- 1 green chili, finely chopped
- 2 garlic cloves, minced
- 10 ml light soy sauce
- Salt and ground black pepper, to taste

DIRECTIONS:

1. Push in the legs on the Cook & Crisp tray, then place the tray in the bottom of the pot. Spray the tray with cooking spray.
2. Place flour in a shallow dish and whisk the eggs, garlic, green chili, soy sauce, salt, and black pepper in a second dish.
3. Coat the cod fillets evenly in flour and dip in the egg mixture.
4. Close the lid and flip the SmartSwitch to AIR FRY/HOB. Select AIRFRY, set temperature to 190°C, and set time to 13 minutes (unit will need to preheat for 5 minutes, so set an external timer if desired). Press START/STOP to begin cooking.
5. When the unit is preheated and the time reaches 8 minutes, place the cod pieces on the tray. Close the lid to begin cooking.
6. After 4 minutes, open the lid and toss the cod pieces with silicone-tipped tongs to ensure even cooking. Close the lid to continue cooking.
7. When cooking is complete, serve warm.

Tuna Patty Sliders

Prep: 15 minutes, Total Cook Time: 12 minutes, Serves: 4

INGREDIENTS:

- Cooking spray
- 10 whole-wheat slider buns
- 3 (140-g) tins tuna, packed in water
- 150 g whole-wheat panko bread crumbs
- 40 g shredded Parmesan cheese
- 15 ml sriracha
- ¾ tsp. black pepper

DIRECTIONS:

1. Push in the legs on the Cook & Crisp tray, then place the tray in the bottom of the pot. Spray the tray with cooking spray.
2. In a medium bowl, mix the tuna, bread crumbs, Parmesan cheese, sriracha, and black pepper and stir to combine well.
3. Shape the mixture into 10 patties.
4. Close the lid and flip the SmartSwitch to AIR FRY/HOB. Select BAKE & ROAST, set temperature to 180°C, and set time to 17 minutes (unit will need to preheat for 5 minutes, so set an external timer if desired). Press START/STOP to begin cooking.
5. When the unit is preheated and the time reaches 12 minutes, place half the patties on the tray, working in batches. Close the lid to begin cooking.
6. After 6 minutes, open the lid. Flip the patties over and lightly spray with cooking spray. Close the lid to continue cooking, until golden brown and crisp.
7. Serve the patties on buns.

Panko Salmon Patties

Prep: 10 minutes, Total Cook Time: 10 minutes, Serves: 4

INGREDIENTS:
- Cooking spray
- 2 (210 g) tins of salmon, flaked
- 2 large eggs, beaten
- 80 g panko bread crumbs
- 50 g minced onion
- 1½ tsps. Italian herb seasoning
- 1 tsp. garlic powder

DIRECTIONS:
1. Push in the legs on the Cook & Crisp tray, then place the tray in the bottom of the pot. Line the tray with parchment paper.
2. Stir together the salmon, eggs, and onion in a medium bowl.
3. Whisk the bread crumbs, Italian herb seasoning, and garlic powder in a small bowl until blended well. Place the bread crumb mixture to the salmon mixture and stir well until blended. Form the mixture into 8 patties.
4. Close the lid and flip the SmartSwitch to AIR FRY/HOB. Select BAKE & ROAST, set temperature to 180°C, and set time to 15 minutes (unit will need to preheat for 5 minutes, so set an external timer if desired). Press START/STOP to begin cooking.
5. When the unit is preheated and the time reaches 10 minutes, place half the patties on the tray, working in batches. Close the lid to begin cooking.
6. After 5 minutes, open the lid. Flip the patties over and lightly spritz with cooking spray. Close the lid to continue cooking, until browned and firm.
7. Serve hot.

Bacon-Wrapped Prawn

Prep: 15 minutes, Total Cook Time: 12 minutes, Steam: approx. 4 minutes, Cook: 8 minutes, Serves: 6

INGREDIENTS:
- 125 ml water, for steaming
- 450 g streaky bacon, thinly sliced
- 450 g prawn, peeled and deveined
- Salt, to taste

DIRECTIONS:
1. Pour 125 ml water into the pot. Push in the legs on the Cook & Crisp tray, then place the tray in the bottom position in the pot.
2. Wrap prawn with salt and a streaky bacon, covering completely.
3. Repeat with the remaining prawn and streaky bacon.
4. Arrange the bacon-wrapped prawns in a baking dish and freeze for about 15 minutes.
5. Place the prawns on the tray.
6. Close the lid and flip the SmartSwitch to RAPID COOKER. Select STEAM AIR FRY, set temperature to 200°C, and set time to 8 minutes. Press START/STOP to begin cooking (the unit will steam for approx. 4 minutes, before countdown time begins).
7. When the time is up, dish out and serve warm.

Easy Roasted Salmon

Prep Time: 5 minutes, Cook Time: 10 minutes, Serves: 2

INGREDIENTS:
- cooking spray
- 2 (170 g) salmon fillets
- Salt and black pepper, as required
- 15 ml olive oil

DIRECTIONS:
1. Push in the legs on the Cook & Crisp tray, then place the tray in the bottom of the pot. Spray the tray with cooking spray.
2. Season each salmon fillet with salt and black pepper and drizzle with olive oil.
3. Close the lid and flip the SmartSwitch to AIR FRY/HOB. Select BAKE & ROAST, set temperature to 200°C, and set time to 15 minutes (unit will need to preheat for 5 minutes, so set an external timer if desired). Press START/STOP to begin cooking.
4. When the unit is preheated and the time reaches 10 minutes, place the salmon fillets on the tray. Close the lid to begin cooking.
5. After 5 minutes, open the lid and toss the salmon fillets with silicone-tipped tongs to ensure even cooking. Close the lid to continue cooking.
6. Dish out the salmon fillets onto the serving plates.

Scallops with Capers Sauce

Prep: 15 minutes, Total Cook Time: 10 minutes, Steam: approx. 4 minutes, Cook: 6 minutes, Serves: 2

INGREDIENTS:
- 60 ml water, for steaming
- 10 (30 g each) sea scallops, cleaned and patted very dry
- 2 tbsps. fresh parsley, finely chopped
- 2 tsps. capers, finely chopped
- Salt and ground black pepper, to taste
- 60 ml extra-virgin olive oil
- 1 tsp. fresh lemon zest, finely grated
- ½ tsp. garlic, finely chopped

DIRECTIONS:
1. Pour 60 ml water into the pot. Pull out the legs on the Cook & Crisp tray, then place the tray in the top position in the pot.
2. Season the scallops evenly with salt and black pepper. Arrange the scallops on the tray.
3. Close the lid and flip the SmartSwitch to RAPID COOKER. Select STEAM AIR FRY, set temperature to 220°C, and set time to 6 minutes. Press START/STOP to begin cooking (the unit will steam for approx. 4 minutes, before countdown time begins).
4. Mix parsley, capers, olive oil, lemon zest and garlic in a bowl.
5. Dish out the scallops in a platter and top with capers sauce.

Mediterranean Cod and Veggies

Prep: 20 minutes, Total Cook Time: 19 minutes, Steam: approx. 4 minutes, Cook: 15 minutes, Serves: 4

INGREDIENTS:

- 125 ml water, for steaming
- 30 g butter, melted
- 50 g red bell peppers, seeded and thinly sliced
- 50 g carrots, peeled and julienned
- 50 g fennel bulbs, julienned
- 2 (140 g) frozen cod fillets, thawed
- 15 ml fresh lemon juice
- ½ tsp. dried tarragon
- Salt and ground black pepper, as required
- 15 ml olive oil

DIRECTIONS:

1. Pour 125 ml water into the pot. Pull out the legs on the Cook & Crisp tray, then place the tray in the top position in the pot.
2. Mix butter, lemon juice, tarragon, salt, and black pepper in a large bowl.
3. Add the carrot, bell pepper and fennel bulb and generously coat with the butter mixture.
4. Coat the cod fillets with olive oil and season with salt and black pepper.
5. Arrange cod fillets on the tray and top evenly with the vegetables. Top with any remaining sauce from the bowl.
6. Close the lid and flip the SmartSwitch to RAPID COOKER. Select STEAM AIR FRY, set temperature to 220°C, and set time to 15 minutes. Press START/STOP to begin cooking (the unit will steam for approx. 4 minutes, before countdown time begins).
7. When cooking is complete, use tongs to remove the cod and veggies from the tray. Serve warm.

Salmon and Veggies Ratatouille

Prep Time: 20 minutes, Cook Time: 6½ hours, Serves: 8

INGREDIENTS:

- 30 ml olive oil
- 900 g salmon fillets
- 5 large tomatoes, seeded and chopped
- 2 aubergines, peeled and chopped
- 150 g sliced button mushrooms
- 2 red bell peppers, stemmed, seeded, and chopped
- 2 onions, chopped
- 5 garlic cloves, minced
- 1 tsp. dried herbs de Provence

DIRECTIONS:

1. Before getting started, be sure to remove the Cook & Crisp tray.
2. Mix the aubergines, tomatoes, mushrooms, onions, bell peppers, garlic, olive oil, and herbes de Provence in the bottom of the pot.
3. Close the lid and flip the SmartSwitch to AIR FRY/HOB. Select SLOW COOK, set temperature to LOW, and set time to 6 hours. Press START/STOP to begin cooking, until the vegetables are soft.
4. When the time is up, open the lid and place the salmon to the pot. Close the lid and cook on low for another 30 to 40 minutes, or until the salmon flakes when tested with a fork.
5. Serve warm.

Spicy Orange Prawn

Prep Time: 20 minutes, Cook Time: 10 minutes, Serves: 4

INGREDIENTS:

- 80 ml orange juice
- 3 tsps. minced garlic
- 1 tsp. Old Bay seasoning
- ¼ to ½ tsp. cayenne pepper
- 450 g king prawns, peeled and deveined, with tails off
- Cooking spray

DIRECTIONS:

1. In a medium bowl, combine the orange juice, garlic, Old Bay seasoning, and cayenne pepper.
2. Dry the prawns with paper towels to remove excess water.
3. Add the prawns to the marinade and stir to evenly coat. Cover with plastic wrap and place in the refrigerator for 30 minutes so the prawns can soak up the marinade.
4. Push in the legs on the Cook & Crisp tray, then place the tray in the bottom of the pot. Spray the tray with cooking spray.
5. Close the lid and flip the SmartSwitch to AIR FRY/HOB. Select AIRFRY, set temperature to 200°C, and set time to 15 minutes (unit will need to preheat for 5 minutes, so set an external timer if desired). Press START/STOP to begin cooking.
6. When the unit is preheated and the time reaches 10 minutes, place the prawns on the tray. Close the lid to begin cooking.
7. After 5 minutes, open the lid. Flip the prawns and lightly spray with cooking spray. Close the lid to continue cooking.
8. Serve immediately.

Spiced Catfish with Spaghetti

Prep: 15 minutes, Total Cook Time: 25 minutes, Steam: approx. 10 minutes, Cook: 15 minutes, Serves: 4

INGREDIENTS:

LEVEL 1 (BOTTOM OF POT)
- 280 g spaghetti pasta, broken in half
- 750 ml water
- 240 ml tomato sauce

LEVEL 2 (TRAY)
- 4 (170 g) catfish fillets
- 15 ml olive oil
- 30 g cornmeal
- 30 g corn flour
- 10 g garlic
- 10 g salt

TOPPINGS:
- Tzatziki
- Guacamole

DIRECTIONS:

1. Place all Level 1 ingredients in the pot and stir to combine.
2. Pull out the legs on the Cook & Crisp tray, then place the tray in the top position in the pot.
3. Mix the catfish fillets with cornmeal, corn flour, garlic and salt in a bowl.
4. Drizzle with olive oil and arrange catfish fillets on top of the tray.
5. Close the lid and flip the SmartSwitch to RAPID COOKER.
6. Select SPEEDI MEALS, set temperature to 180°C, and set time to 15 minutes. Press START/STOP to begin cooking (the unit will steam for approx. 10 minutes, before countdown time begins).
7. When cooking is complete, remove the catfish fillets from the tray. Then use silicone-tipped tongs to grab the centre handle and remove the tray from the unit. Transfer the spaghetti pasta to a bowl, then top with the catfish fillets and desired toppings.

Savory Tuna Cakes

Prep: 20 minutes, Total Cook Time: 20 minutes, Steam: approx. 8 minutes, Cook: 12 minutes, Serves: 4

INGREDIENTS:

- 250 ml water, for steaming
- 1 onion, chopped
- 2 (170 g) tins of tuna, drained
- 1 medium boiled potato, mashed
- 100 g celery
- 130 g breadcrumbs
- 2 eggs
- 7 ml olive oil
- 1 tbsp. fresh ginger, grated
- Salt, as required

DIRECTIONS:

1. Pour 250 ml water into the pot. Push in the legs on the Cook & Crisp tray, then place the tray in the bottom position in the pot.
2. Heat olive oil in a frying pan and add onions, ginger, and green chili.
3. Sauté for about 30 seconds and add the tuna.
4. Stir fry for about 3 minutes and dish out the tuna mixture onto a large bowl.
5. Add mashed potato, celery, and salt and mix well.
6. Make 4 equal-sized patties from the mixture.
7. Place the breadcrumbs in a shallow bowl and whisk the egg in another bowl.
8. Dredge each patty with breadcrumbs, then dip into egg and coat again with the breadcrumbs. Arrange tuna cakes on the tray.
9. Close the lid and flip the SmartSwitch to RAPID COOKER. Select STEAM BAKE, set temperature to 200°C, and set time to 8 minutes. Press START/STOP to begin cooking (the unit will steam for approx. 8 minutes, before countdown time begins).
10. With 4 minutes remaining, open the lid and flip the side with tongs. Close the lid to continue cooking.
11. Dish out the tuna cakes onto serving plates and serve warm.

Salmon Vegetables Chowder

Prep Time: 15 minutes, Cook Time: 7½ hours, Serves: 8 to 10

INGREDIENTS:

- 900 g skinless salmon fillets
- 6 medium potatoes, cut into 5 cm pieces
- 4 large carrots, sliced
- 350 g sliced chestnut mushrooms
- 170 g shredded Swiss cheese
- 240 ml whole milk
- 2 L vegetable broth or fish stock
- 4 shallots, minced
- 3 garlic cloves, minced
- 2 tsps. dried dill weed

DIRECTIONS:

1. Before getting started, be sure to remove the Cook & Crisp tray.
2. Mix the potatoes, carrots, mushrooms, shallots, garlic, vegetable broth, and dill weed in the bottom of the pot.
3. Close the lid and flip the SmartSwitch to AIR FRY/HOB. Select SLOW COOK, set temperature to LOW, and set time to 7 hours. Press START/STOP to begin cooking, until the vegetables are soft.
4. Place the salmon fillets to the pot. Close the lid and cook on low for an additional 20 to 30 minutes, or until the salmon flakes when tested with a fork.
5. Gently stir the chowder to break up the salmon.
6. Pour in the milk and Swiss cheese and cover. Let the chowder sit for 10 minutes to let the cheese melt. Stir in the chowder and serve warm.

Rice Noodles with Broccoli and Scallop

Prep: 12 minutes, Total Cook Time: 13 to 16 minutes, Steam: approx. 7 to 8 minutes, Cook: 6 to 8 minutes, Serves: 2

INGREDIENTS:

LEVEL 1 (BOTTOM OF POT)
- 1 (400 g) package flat rice noodles
- 340 g fresh broccoli florets, split
- 500 ml water
- 60 ml vegetable oil, plus more as needed
- 1 garlic clove, minced
- 35 ml oyster sauce
- 15 ml light soy sauce
- 1 tbsp. sugar
- 15 ml rice vinegar
- 45 ml sweet, dark soy sauce

LEVEL 2 (TRAY)
- 12 large sea scallops, tendons removed
- Salt and pepper, to taste
- 15 ml cider vinegar
- 1 tsp. Dijon mustard

TOPPINGS (optional)
- lemon wedges

DIRECTIONS:

1. Place all Level 1 ingredients in the pot and stir to combine well.
2. Pull out the legs on the Cook & Crisp tray, then place the tray in the top position in the pot above the noodles.
3. Mix all Level 2 ingredients in a large bowl, then place the scallop on top of the tray in a single layer.
4. Close the lid and flip the SmartSwitch to RAPID COOKER. Select SPEEDI MEALS, set temperature to 200°C, and set time to 6 to 8 minutes. Press START/STOP to begin cooking (the unit will steam for approx. 7 to 8 minutes, before countdown time begins).
5. When cooking is complete, remove the scallop from the tray. Then use silicone tipped tongs to remove the Cook & Crisp tray. Remove the noodles and broccoli. Serve topped with lemon wedges and scallop.

Prawn and Polenta with Tomato

Prep Time: 16 minutes, Cook Time: 6½ hours, Serves: 9

INGREDIENTS:

- 900 g raw prawns, peeled and deveined
- 4 large tomatoes, seeded and chopped
- 440 g polenta
- 2 L chicken stock or vegetable broth
- 2 onions, chopped
- 2 green bell peppers, stemmed, seeded, and chopped
- 170 g shredded Cheddar cheese
- 5 garlic cloves, minced
- 1 bay leaf
- 1 tsp. Old Bay Seasoning

DIRECTIONS:

1. Before getting started, be sure to remove the Cook & Crisp tray.
2. Mix the polenta, onions, garlic, tomatoes, bell peppers, chicken stock, bay leaf, and seasoning in the bottom of the pot.
3. Close the lid and flip the SmartSwitch to AIR FRY/HOB. Select SLOW COOK, set temperature to LOW, and set time to 6 hours. Press START/STOP to begin cooking, until the polenta are soft and most of the liquid is absorbed.
4. When the time is up, open the lid and place the prawns, stirring. Close the lid and cook on low for 30 to 40 minutes, until the prawns are curled and pink.
5. Stir in the cheese and serve warm.

Honey Glazed Salmon with Sweet Potato Rice

Prep: 15 minutes, Total Cook Time: 21 minutes, Steam: approx. 10 minutes, Cook: 11 minutes, Serves: 2

INGREDIENTS:

LEVEL 1 (BOTTOM OF POT)
- 200 g jasmine rice, rinsed
- 200 g fresh sweet potato, chopped
- 500 ml water

LEVEL 2 (TRAY)
- 5 ml water
- 2 (100 g each) salmon fillets
- 80 ml soy sauce
- 80 ml honey
- 3 tsps. rice wine vinegar

DIRECTIONS:

1. Place all Level 1 ingredients in the pot and stir to combine.
2. Pull out the legs on the Cook & Crisp tray, then place the tray in the top position in the pot.
3. Mix all Level 2 ingredients in a small bowl except salmon.
4. Reserve half of the mixture in a small bowl and coat the salmon in remaining mixture.
5. Refrigerate, covered for about 30 minutes and place the salmon on top of the tray.
6. Close the lid and flip the SmartSwitch to RAPID COOKER.
7. Select SPEEDI MEALS, set temperature to 180°C, and set time to 10 minutes. Press START/STOP to begin cooking (the unit will steam for approx. 10 minutes, before countdown time begins).
8. With 5 minutes remaining, open the lid and coat the salmon with reserved marinade. Close the lid to continue cooking.
9. When cooking is complete, remove the salmon from the tray. Then use silicone-tipped tongs to grab the centre handle and remove the tray from the unit. Transfer the rice and sweet potato to a bowl.
10. Place the reserved marinade in a small pan and cook the salmon for about 1 minute.
11. Serve the salmon and sweet potato rice with marinade sauce.

CHAPTER 3
VEGETABLES

Sweet Potato Chips

Prep Time: 5 minutes, Cook Time: 20 minutes, Serves: 4

INGREDIENTS:

- 900 g sweet potatoes, rinsed, sliced into matchsticks
- 1 tsp. curry powder
- cooking spray
- Salt, to taste

DIRECTIONS:

1. Push in the legs on the Cook & Crisp tray, then place the tray in the bottom of the pot. Spray the tray with cooking spray.
2. Close the lid and flip the SmartSwitch to AIR FRY/HOB. Select AIRFRY, set temperature to 200°C, and set time to 25 minutes (unit will need to preheat for 5 minutes, so set an external timer if desired). Press START/STOP to begin cooking.
3. When the unit is preheated and the time reaches 20 minutes, place the chips on the tray. Close the lid to begin cooking.
4. After 15 minutes, open the lid and toss the chips with silicone-tipped tongs to ensure even cooking. Close the lid to continue cooking.
5. When cooking is complete, sprinkle with the curry powder and salt before serving.

Italian Aubergine Slices

Prep Time: 10 minutes, Cook Time: 8 minutes, Serves: 2

INGREDIENTS:

- Cooking spray
- 1 medium aubergine, peeled and cut into 1.3 cm round slices
- 65 g plain flour
- 100 g Italian-style breadcrumbs
- 2 eggs, beaten
- 30 ml milk
- Salt, to taste
- 60 ml olive oil

DIRECTIONS:

1. Push in the legs on the Cook & Crisp tray, then place the tray in the bottom of the pot. Spray the tray with cooking spray.
2. Season the aubergine slices with salt and keep aside for 1 hour.
3. Place flour in a shallow dish.
4. Whisk the eggs with milk in a second dish.
5. Mix together oil and breadcrumbs in a third shallow dish.
6. Coat the aubergine slices evenly with flour, then dip in the egg mixture and finally coat with breadcrumb mixture.
7. Close the lid and flip the SmartSwitch to AIR FRY/HOB. Select AIRFRY, set temperature to 200°C, and set time to 13 minutes (unit will need to preheat for 5 minutes, so set an external timer if desired). Press START/STOP to begin cooking.
8. When the unit is preheated and the time reaches 8 minutes, place the aubergine slices on the tray. Close the lid to begin cooking.
9. When cooking is complete, serve hot.

Cheese Stuffed Tomatoes

Prep: 15 minutes, Total Cook Time: 19 minutes, Steam: approx. 4 minutes, Cook: 15 minutes, Serves: 2

INGREDIENTS:

- 250 ml water, for steaming
- cooking spray
- 2 large tomatoes, sliced in half and pulp scooped out
- 50 g broccoli, finely chopped
- 50 g cheddar cheese, grated
- 15 g unsalted butter, melted
- ½ tsp. dried thyme, crushed

DIRECTIONS:

1. Pour 250 ml water into the pot. Push in the legs on the Cook & Crisp tray, then place the tray in the bottom position in the pot. Spray Multi-Purpose Tin or 20cm cake tin with cooking spray.
2. Mix together broccoli and cheese in a bowl.
3. Stuff the broccoli mixture in each tomato.
4. Arrange the stuffed tomatoes to the prepared tin and drizzle evenly with butter. Then place the tin on the tray.
5. Close the lid and flip the SmartSwitch to RAPID COOKER. Select STEAM AIR FRY, set temperature to 180°C, and set time to 15 minutes. Press START/STOP to begin cooking (the unit will approx. 4 minutes, before countdown time begins).
6. Dish out in a serving platter.
7. Garnish with thyme and serve warm.

Crispy Cornmeal Okra

Prep Time: 5 minutes, Cook Time: 10 minutes, Serves: 4

INGREDIENTS:

- Cooking spray
- 150 g self-raising cornmeal
- 1 tsp. Italian-style seasoning
- 1 tsp. Paprika
- 1 tsp. salt
- ½ tsp. freshly ground black pepper
- 2 large eggs, beaten
- 250 g okra slices

DIRECTIONS:

1. Push in the legs on the Cook & Crisp tray, then place the tray in the bottom of the pot. Spray the tray with cooking spray.
2. In a shallow bowl, whisk the cornmeal, Italian-style seasoning, paprika, salt, and pepper until blended. Place the beaten eggs in a second shallow bowl.
3. Add the okra to the beaten egg and stir to coat. Add the egg and okra mixture to the cornmeal mixture and stir until coated.
4. Close the lid and flip the SmartSwitch to AIR FRY/HOB. Select AIRFRY, set temperature to 200°C, and set time to 15 minutes (unit will need to preheat for 5 minutes, so set an external timer if desired). Press START/STOP to begin cooking.
5. When the unit is preheated and the time reaches 10 minutes, place the okra on the tray. Close the lid to begin cooking.
6. After 5 minutes, open the lid and toss the okra with silicone-tipped tongs to ensure even cooking. Spritz the okra with cooking spray. Close the lid to continue cooking, until lightly browned and crispy.
7. When cooking is complete, serve hot.

CHAPTER 3: VEGETABLES

Blistered Shishito Peppers

Prep: 10 minutes, Total Cook Time: 8 minutes, Serves: 4

INGREDIENTS:

For the Dipping Sauce:
- 240 ml sour cream
- 1 spring onion (white and green parts), finely chopped
- 1 clove garlic, minced
- 30 ml fresh lemon juice

For the Peppers:
- 225 g shishito peppers
- 15 ml vegetable oil
- 5 ml toasted sesame oil
- ½ tsp. toasted sesame seeds
- ¼ to ½ tsp. red pepper flakes
- Coarse salt and black pepper, to taste

DIRECTIONS:

1. Push in the legs on the Cook & Crisp tray, then place the tray in the bottom of the pot. Spray the tray with cooking spray.
2. In a small bowl, mix all the ingredients for the dipping sauce to combine well. Cover and refrigerate until serving time.
3. In a medium bowl, stir the peppers with the vegetable oil.
4. Close the lid and flip the SmartSwitch to AIR FRY/HOB. Select AIRFRY, set temperature to 180°C, and set time to 13 minutes (unit will need to preheat for 5 minutes, so set an external timer if desired). Press START/STOP to begin cooking.
5. When the unit is preheated and the time reaches 8 minutes, place the peppers on the tray. Close the lid to begin cooking.
6. After 4 minutes, open the lid and toss the peppers with silicone-tipped tongs to ensure even cooking. Close the lid to continue cooking.
7. When cooking is complete, transfer the peppers to a serving bowl. Pour the sesame oil and toss to coat well. Sprinkle with salt and pepper. Place the red pepper and sesame seeds and toss again.
8. Serve hot with the dipping sauce.

Braised Sweet and Sour Red Cabbage

Prep Time: 15 minutes, Cook Time: 6 hours, Serves: 6 to 8

INGREDIENTS:

- 1 medium head red cabbage, cored and chopped (about 560 g)
- 1 Granny Smith apple, peeled and chopped
- 1 red onion, chopped
- 60 ml apple cider vinegar
- 60 g honey
- Pinch ground cloves
- ½ tsp. salt
- ⅛ tsp. freshly ground black pepper

DIRECTIONS:

1. Before getting started, be sure to remove the Cook & Crisp tray.
2. Mix all the ingredients in the bottom of the pot.
3. Close the lid and flip the SmartSwitch to AIR FRY/HOB. Select SLOW COOK, set temperature to LOW, and set time to 6 hours. Press START/STOP to begin cooking, until the cabbage is soft.
4. Serve warm.

French Green Beans with Shallot

Prep: 10 minutes, Total Cook Time: 14 minutes, Steam: approx. 4 minutes, Cook: 10 minutes, Serves: 4

INGREDIENTS:

- 125 ml water, for steaming
- 30 ml olive oil
- 680 g French green beans, stems removed and blanched
- 225 shallots, peeled and cut into quarters
- 1 tbsp. salt
- ½ tsp. ground white pepper

DIRECTIONS:

1. Pour 125 ml water into the pot. Push in the legs on the Cook & Crisp tray, then place the tray in the bottom position in the pot.
2. Coat the vegetables evenly with the rest of the ingredients in a bowl. Then transfer the vegetables to the tray.
3. Close the lid and flip the SmartSwitch to RAPID COOKER. Select STEAM AIR FRY, set temperature to 190°C, and set time to 10 minutes. Press START/STOP to begin cooking (the unit will steam for approx. 4 minutes, before countdown time begins).
4. With 5 minutes remaining, open the lid and toss the vegetables with tongs. Close the lid to continue cooking.
5. When cooking is complete, use tongs to remove the vegetables from the tray and serve hot.

Roasted Potatoes and Asparagus

Prep Time: 5 minutes, Cook Time: 38 minutes, Serves: 4

INGREDIENTS:

- Cook spray
- 4 medium potatoes
- 1 bunch asparagus
- 80 g cottage cheese
- 80 g low-fat crème fraiche
- 1 tbsp. wholegrain mustard
- Salt and pepper, to taste

DIRECTIONS:

1. Push in the legs on the Cook & Crisp tray, then place the tray in the bottom of the pot. Spray the tray with cooking spray.
2. Close the lid and flip the SmartSwitch to AIR FRY/HOB. Select BAKE & ROAST, set temperature to 200°C, and set time to 40 minutes (unit will need to preheat for 5 minutes, so set an external timer if desired). Press START/STOP to begin cooking.
3. When the unit is preheated and the time reaches 35 minutes, place the potatoes on the tray. Close the lid to begin cooking.
4. Meanwhile, boil the asparagus in salted water for 3 minutes.
5. After 20 minutes, open the lid and flip the potatoes with silicone-tipped tongs to ensure even cooking. Close the lid to continue cooking.
6. When cooking is complete, remove the potatoes and mash them with rest of ingredients except the asparagus. Sprinkle with salt and pepper.
7. Serve the mashed potato and asparagus.

Vegetable Ratatouille

Prep: 20 minutes, Total Cook Time: 22 minutes, Serves: 4

INGREDIENTS:

- Cooking spray
- 1 sprig basil
- 1 sprig flat-leaf parsley
- 1 sprig mint
- 1 tbsp. coriander powder
- 1 tsp. capers
- Juice of ½ lemon
- 2 aubergines, sliced crosswise
- 2 red onions, chopped
- 4 cloves garlic, minced
- 75 ml olive oil
- 2 red peppers, chopped
- 1 fennel bulb, sliced crosswise
- 3 large courgettes, sliced crosswise
- 4 large tomatoes, sliced crosswise
- 2 tsps. herbs de Provence
- Salt and ground black pepper, to taste

DIRECTIONS:

1. Push in the legs on the Cook & Crisp tray, then place the tray in the bottom of the pot. Spray Multi-Purpose Tin or 20cm cake tin with cooking spray.
2. Blend the basil, parsley, coriander, mint, lemon juice and capers, with a pinch of salt and pepper. Make sure all the ingredients are well-incorporated.
3. Coat the aubergines, onions, peppers, fennel, garlic, and courgettes with olive oil.
4. Close the lid and flip the SmartSwitch to AIR FRY/HOB. Select AIRFRY, set temperature to 200°C, and set time to 27 minutes (unit will need to preheat for 5 minutes, so set an external timer if desired). Press START/STOP to begin cooking.
5. When the unit is preheated and the time reaches 22 minutes, place the vegetables in the pan, then transfer to the tray. Top with the tomatoes and herb purée. Season with more salt and pepper, and the herbs de Provence. Close the lid to begin cooking.
6. After 10 minutes, open the lid and toss the vegetables with silicone-tipped tongs to ensure even cooking. Close the lid to continue cooking.
7. When cooking is complete, serve immediately.

Brussels Sprouts

Prep Time: 20 minutes, Cook Time: 8 hours, Serves: 6

INGREDIENTS:

- 450 g Brussels sprouts, trimmed and removed any wilted leaves

DIRECTIONS:

1. Boil or steam whole Brussels sprouts until you can pierce them with a sharp knife or skewer. Drain and place the sprouts in a large bowl of ice water until cool. Cut each sprout vertically in half through the stem and spread on dehydrator rack, cut side up.
2. Push in the legs on the Cook & Crisp tray, then place the tray in the bottom position in the pot. Put the rack with Brussels sprouts on the tray.
3. Close the lid and flip the SmartSwitch to AIR FRY/HOB. Select DEHYDRATE, set temperature to 60°C, and set time to 8 hours. Press START/STOP to begin cooking. When done, the Brussels sprouts should feel dry to the touch and be crunchy.
4. Remove the Brussels sprouts from the cooker, serve immediately ou vacuum seal in vacuum bags with an oxygen pack, and then double-bagged in Mylar bag.

Sweet Potatoes with Carrot

Prep: 20 minutes, Total Cook Time: 24 minutes, Steam: approx. 4 minutes, Cook: 20 minutes, Serves: 4

INGREDIENTS:

- 125 ml water, for steaming
- 2 large-sized sweet potatoes, peeled and quartered
- 1 medium courgette, sliced
- 1 Serrano pepper, deseeded and thinly sliced
- 1 bell pepper, deseeded and thinly sliced
- 1 to 2 carrots, cut into matchsticks
- 60 ml olive oil
- 20 ml maple syrup
- ½ tsp. porcini powder
- ¼ tsp. mustard powder
- ½ tsp. fennel seeds
- 1 tbsp. garlic powder
- ½ tsp. fine sea salt
- ¼ tsp. ground black pepper
- Tomato ketchup, for serving

DIRECTIONS:

1. Pour 125 ml water into the pot. Push in the legs on the Cook & Crisp tray, then place the tray in the bottom position in the pot.
2. Put the sweet potatoes, courgette, peppers, and the carrot on the tray. Coat with a drizzling of olive oil.
3. Close the lid and flip the SmartSwitch to RAPID COOKER. Select STEAM AIR FRY, set temperature to 220°C, and set time to 20 minutes. Press START/STOP to begin cooking (the unit will steam for approx. 4 minutes, before countdown time begins).
4. In the meantime, prepare the sauce by vigorously combining the other ingredients, except for the tomato ketchup, with a whisk.
5. With 5 minutes remaining, open the lid and toss the vegetables with tongs. Pour over the sauce and coat the vegetables well. Close the lid to continue cooking.
6. When cooking is complete, serve warm with a side of ketchup.

Garlic Root Vegetable Hash

Prep Time: 18 minutes, Cook Time: 8 hours, Serves: 8

INGREDIENTS:

- 30 ml olive oil
- 4 medium-sized potatoes, chopped
- 3 large carrots, peeled and chopped
- 2 large russet potatoes, chopped
- 1 large parsnip, peeled and chopped
- 2 onions, chopped
- 2 garlic cloves, minced
- 60 ml vegetable broth
- 1 tsp. dried thyme leaves
- ½ tsp. salt

DIRECTIONS:

1. Before getting started, be sure to remove the Cook & Crisp tray.
2. Mix all the ingredients in the bottom of the pot.
3. Close the lid and flip the SmartSwitch to AIR FRY/HOB. Select SLOW COOK, set temperature to LOW, and set time to 8 hours. Press START/STOP to begin cooking.
4. Stir the hash well and serve warm.

Honey-Glazed Parsnips, Carrots and Fennel

Prep Time: 10 minutes, Cook Time: 7 hours, Serves: 8 to 10

INGREDIENTS:

- 4 medium parsnips, peeled and cut into 5-cm pieces
- 4 medium carrots, peeled and cut into 5-cm pieces
- 1 fennel bulb, cored and chopped
- 60 ml honey
- 60 ml vegetable broth
- 2 garlic cloves, minced
- ½ tsp. salt

DIRECTIONS:

1. Before getting started, be sure to remove the Cook & Crisp tray.
2. Mix all of the ingredients in the bottom of the pot.
3. Close the lid and flip the SmartSwitch to AIR FRY/HOB. Select SLOW COOK, set temperature to LOW, and set time to 7 hours. Press START/STOP to begin cooking, until the vegetables are tender when pierced with a fork.
4. Serve warm.

Curried Winter Squash

Prep Time: 17 minutes, Cook Time: 6 hours, Serves: 6 to 8

INGREDIENTS:

- 3 acorn squashes, peeled, seeded, and cut into 2.5 cm pieces
- 1 large butternut squash, peeled, seeded, and cut into 2.5 cm pieces
- 80 ml freshly squeezed orange juice
- 2 onions, finely chopped
- 5 garlic cloves, minced
- 1 tbsp. curry powder
- ½ tsp. salt

DIRECTIONS:

1. Before getting started, be sure to remove the Cook & Crisp tray.
2. Mix all of the ingredients in the bottom of the pot.
3. Close the lid and flip the SmartSwitch to AIR FRY/HOB. Select SLOW COOK, set temperature to LOW, and set time to 6 hours. Press START/STOP to begin cooking, until the winter squash is tender when pierced with a fork.
4. Serve warm.

Rosemary White Beans with Onion

Prep Time: 8 minutes, Cook Time: 8 hours, Serves: 16

INGREDIENTS:

- 450g dried haricot or cannellini beans
- 500 ml low sodium vegetable broth
- 1 L water
- 1 onion, finely chopped
- 3 cloves garlic, minced
- 1 large sprig fresh rosemary
- ½ tsp. salt
- ⅛ tsp. white pepper

DIRECTIONS:

1. Before getting started, be sure to remove the Cook & Crisp tray.
2. Sort over the beans, remove and discard any extraneous material. Rinse the beans well over cold water and drain.
3. Mix the beans, onion, garlic, rosemary, salt, water, and vegetable broth in the bottom of the pot.
4. Close the lid and flip the SmartSwitch to AIR FRY/HOB. Select SLOW COOK, set temperature to LOW, and set time to 8 hours. Press START/STOP to begin cooking, until the beans are soft.
5. Remove and discard the rosemary stem. Stir in the mixture gently and serve warm.

Buttered Sweetcorn on the Cob

Prep: 10 minutes, Total Cook Time: 28 minutes, Steam: approx. 8 minutes, Cook: 20 minutes, Serves: 2

INGREDIENTS:

- 125 ml water, for steaming
- 2 sweetcorn on the cob
- 30 g butter, softened and divided
- Salt and black pepper, to taste

DIRECTIONS:

1. Pour 125 ml water into the pot. Push in the legs on the Cook & Crisp tray, then place the tray in the bottom position in the pot.
2. Season the cobs evenly with salt and black pepper and rub with 15 g butter.
3. Wrap the cobs in foil paper and arrange on the tray.
4. Close the lid and flip the SmartSwitch to RAPID COOKER. Select STEAM AIR FRY, set temperature to 160°C, and set time to 20 minutes. Press START/STOP to begin cooking (the unit will steam for approx. 8 minutes, before countdown time begins).
5. When cooking is complete, top with remaining butter. Serve warm.

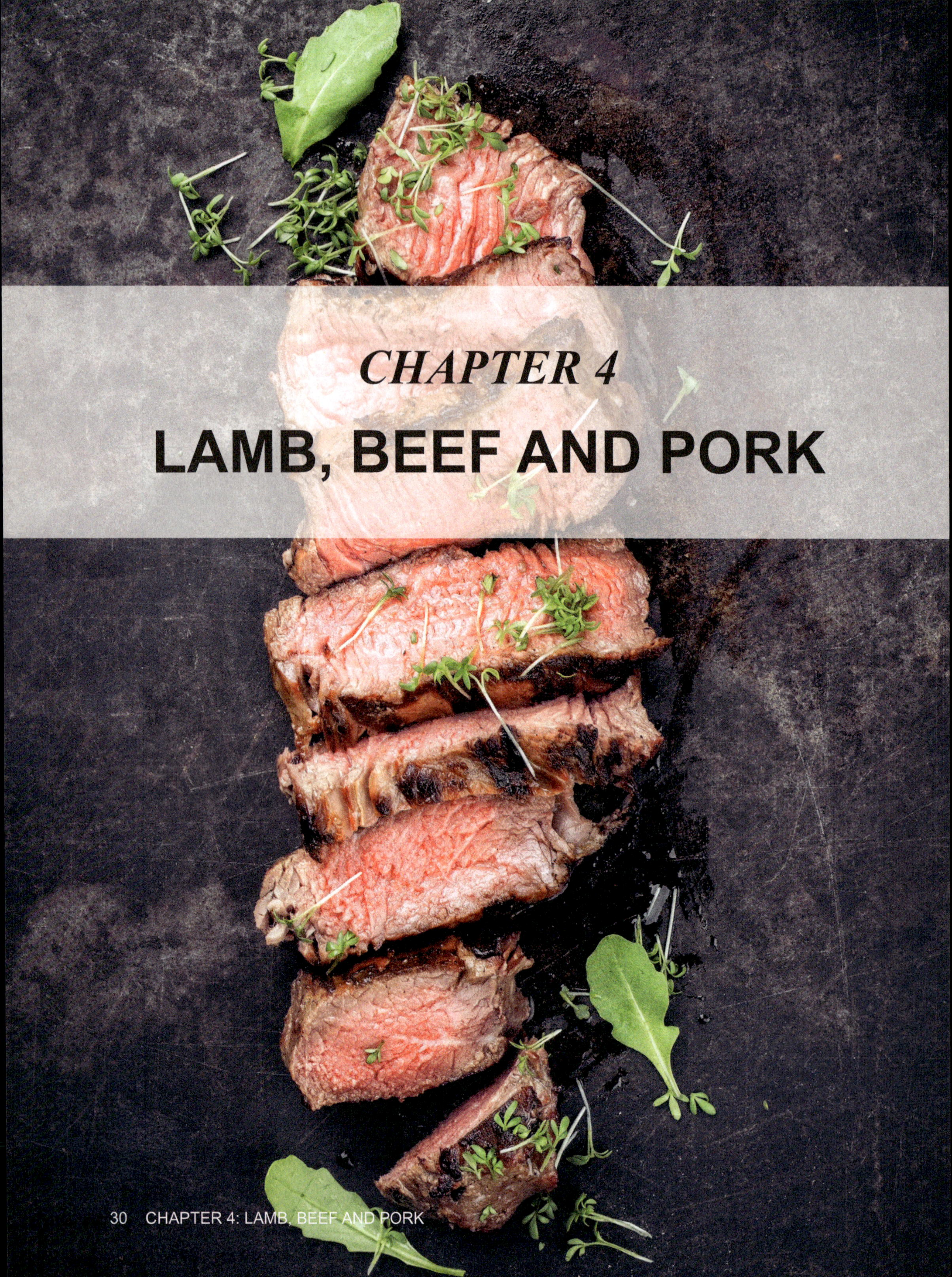

CHAPTER 4
LAMB, BEEF AND PORK

Classic Sweet and Sour Pork and Pineapple

Prep Time: 15 minutes, Cook Time: 6 minutes, Serves: 5

INGREDIENTS:

- 450 g pork tenderloin, cut into 2.5 cm pieces
- 1 (225-g) tin pineapple chunks, drained, juice reserved
- 1 red bell pepper, cut into 2.5 cm pieces
- 1 medium red onion, cut into 2.5 cm pieces
- 4 scallions, cut into 2.5 cm pieces
- 2 garlic cloves, crushed and chopped
- 60 ml cooking oil
- 45 g cornflour, divided
- 60 ml rice vinegar
- 25 g brown sugar
- 1 tbsp. ginger, crushed and chopped

DIRECTIONS:

1. Whisk together the reserved pineapple juice, rice vinegar, 10 g of the cornflour, and brown sugar in a small bowl. Set aside.
2. Put the pork to a resealable plastic bag or covered bowl. Toss with the remaining 35 g of cornflour to coat fully.
3. Before getting started, be sure to remove the Cook & Crisp tray from the pot.
4. Flip the SmartSwitch to AIR FRY/HOB. Select SEAR/SAUTÉ and set to HI-5. Press START/STOP to begin cooking.
5. Heat the cooking oil in the pot until it shimmers.
6. Add the garlic and ginger and sear for about 1 minute.
7. Place the pork and shallow-fry until lightly browned. Remove the pork and keep aside.
8. Remove and discard all but 30 ml of oil from the pot.
9. Arrange the onion to the pot and sauté for 1 minute.
10. Then put the bell pepper and pineapple chunks and sauté for 1 minute.
11. Pour in the pineapple juice mixture and stir until a glaze is formed. Stir in the cooked pork.
12. Sprinkle with the scallions and serve warm.

Citrus Roasted Pork

Prep Time: 10 minutes, Cook Time: 35 minutes, Serves: 8

INGREDIENTS:

- 15 ml lime juice
- 1 tbsp. orange marmalade
- 1 tsp. coarse brown mustard
- 1 tsp. curry powder
- 1 tsp. dried lemongrass
- 900 g boneless pork loin roast
- Salt and ground black pepper, to taste
- Cooking spray

DIRECTIONS:

1. Push in the legs on the Cook & Crisp tray, then place the tray in the bottom of the pot. Spray the tray with cooking spray.
2. Mix the lime juice, marmalade, mustard, curry powder, and lemongrass.
3. Rub mixture all over the surface of the pork loin. Season with salt and pepper.
4. Wrap roast in foil and let rest for 10 minutes before slicing.
5. Close the lid and flip the SmartSwitch to AIR FRY/HOB. Select BAKE & ROAST, set temperature to 190°C, and set time to 40 minutes (unit will need to preheat for 5 minutes, so set an external timer if desired). Press START/STOP to begin cooking.
6. When the unit is preheated and the time reaches 35 minutes, place the pork roast diagonally on the tray. Close the lid to begin cooking.
7. After 20 minutes, open the lid and flip the pork roast with silicone-tipped tongs to ensure even cooking. Close the lid to continue cooking, until the internal temperature reaches at least 63ºC.

CHAPTER 4: LAMB, BEEF AND PORK   31

Gourmet Meatloaf

Prep Time: 15 minutes, Cook Time: 25 minutes, Serves: 4

INGREDIENTS:

- cooking spray
- 400 g lean beef, minced
- 1 chorizo sausage, chopped finely
- 1 small onion, chopped
- 20 g breadcrumbs
- 15 g fresh mushrooms, sliced thinly
- 1 garlic clove, minced
- Salt and black pepper, to taste
- 30 ml olive oil

DIRECTIONS:

1. Push in the legs on the Cook & Crisp tray, then place the tray in the bottom of the pot. Spray a baking pan with cooking spray.
2. Mix all the ingredients in a large bowl except mushrooms.
3. Place the beef mixture in the pan and smooth the surface with the back of spatula.
4. Top with mushroom slices and press into the meatloaf gently. Drizzle evenly with oil.
5. Close the lid and flip the SmartSwitch to AIR FRY/HOB. Select BAKE & ROAST, set temperature to 200°C, and set time to 30 minutes (unit will need to preheat for 5 minutes, so set an external timer if desired). Press START/STOP to begin cooking.
6. When the unit is preheated and the time reaches 25 minutes, place the pan on the tray. Close the lid to begin cooking.
7. Cut into desires size wedges to serve.

Sweet and Spicy Pepper Beef Jerky

Prep Time: 20 minutes, Cook Time: 6 hours 15 minutes, Makes: 225 g jerky

INGREDIENTS:

- 680 g beef eye of round
- 120 ml pineapple juice
- 50 g firmly packed brown sugar
- 60 ml soy sauce
- 1 tbsp. crushed dehydrated jalapeños
- 5 ml hot sauce

DIRECTIONS:

1. Trim the meat of any visible fat, then partially freeze. Cut into 0.5-cm-thick slices or strips across the grain using a very sharp knife or meat slicer. Try to cut the meat as uniformly as possible for even drying. Place the strips in a large ziptop plastic freezer bag.
2. While the meat freezes, combine the remaining ingredients in a small saucepan. Place over medium heat and stir until the sugar dissolves. Let cool, then carefully pour over the strips in the bag. Squish everything around to coat, then seal the bag and refrigerate until the meat is no longer red, about 24 hours, turning and squishing the bag about halfway through to ensure even coverage with the marinade.
3. Drain off the marinade and place the strips in a single layer on dehydrator rack.
4. Push in the legs on the Cook & Crisp tray, then place the tray in the bottom position in the pot. Put the rack with jerk on the tray.
5. Close the lid and flip the SmartSwitch to AIR FRY/HOB. Select DEHYDRATE, set temperature to 70°C, and set time to 6 hours. Press START/STOP to begin cooking. When done, the jerky should bend but not snap, and show no signs of redness.
6. Remove the jerky from the cooker, arrange on baking sheets in a single layer, and place in a preheated 135°C oven for 15 minutes. Allow the jerky to cool completely before placing in an airtight container.

Beef Roast with Mushroom and Carrot

Prep Time: 16 minutes, Cook Time: 10 hours, Serves: 8 to 10

INGREDIENTS:

- 30 g butter
- 1 (1.4-kg) grass-fed chuck shoulder roast or tri-tip roast, cut into 5 cm pieces
- 5 large carrots, sliced
- 200 g sliced chestnut mushrooms
- 250 ml low-sodium beef broth
- 2 onions, sliced
- 4 garlic cloves, sliced
- 2 shallots, peeled and sliced
- 6 g chopped fresh chives
- 1 tsp. dried marjoram leaves

DIRECTIONS:

1. Before getting started, be sure to remove the Cook & Crisp tray.
2. Mix the onions, garlic, shallots, mushrooms, and carrots in the bottom of the pot.
3. Place the beef and stir slowly. Scatter the chives and marjoram over the beef, and add the beef broth over all.
4. Close the lid and flip the SmartSwitch to AIR FRY/HOB. Select SLOW COOK, set temperature to LOW, and set time to 10 hours. Press START/STOP to begin cooking, until the beef is very soft.
5. Stir in the butter and serve warm.

Tasty Beef Roast

Prep Time: 10 minutes, Cook Time: 40 minutes, Serves: 5

INGREDIENTS:

- cooking spray
- 900 g beef roast
- 15 ml olive oil
- 1 tsp. dried rosemary, crushed
- 1 tsp. dried thyme, crushed
- Salt, to taste

DIRECTIONS:

1. Push in the legs on the Cook & Crisp tray, then place the tray in the bottom of the pot. Spray the tray with cooking spray.
2. Rub the roast generously with herb mixture and coat with olive oil.
3. Close the lid and flip the SmartSwitch to AIR FRY/HOB. Select BAKE & ROAST, set temperature to 180°C, and set time to 45 minutes (unit will need to preheat for 5 minutes, so set an external timer if desired). Press START/STOP to begin cooking.
4. When the unit is preheated and the time reaches 40 minutes, place the roast on the tray. Close the lid to begin cooking.
5. After 20 minutes, open the lid and turn the roast over with silicone-tipped tongs to ensure even cooking. Close the lid to continue cooking.
6. Dish out the roast and cover with foil for about 10 minutes.
7. Cut into desired size slices and serve.

Roasted Lamb Leg

Prep Time: 15 minutes, Cook Time: 40 minutes, Serves: 4

INGREDIENTS:

- cooking spray
- 1.1 kg half lamb leg roast, slits carved
- 2 garlic cloves, sliced into smaller slithers
- 1 tbsp. dried rosemary
- 15 ml olive oil
- Cracked Himalayan rock salt and cracked peppercorns, to taste

DIRECTIONS:

1. Push in the legs on the Cook & Crisp tray, then place the tray in the bottom of the pot. Spray the tray with cooking spray.
2. Insert the garlic slithers in the slits and brush with rosemary, oil, salt, and black pepper.
3. Close the lid and flip the SmartSwitch to AIR FRY/HOB. Select BAKE & ROAST, set temperature to 200°C, and set time to 45 minutes (unit will need to preheat for 5 minutes, so set an external timer if desired). Press START/STOP to begin cooking.
4. When the unit is preheated and the time reaches 40 minutes, place the lamb on the tray. Close the lid to begin cooking.
5. Dish out the lamb and serve hot.

Mustard Lamb Ribs

Prep: 5 minutes, Total Cook Time: 18 minutes, Serves: 4

INGREDIENTS:

- cooking spray
- 450 g lamb ribs
- 30 ml mustard
- 240 ml Green yogurt
- 10 g mint leaves, chopped
- 1 tsp. rosemary, chopped
- Salt and ground black pepper, to taste

DIRECTIONS:

1. Push in the legs on the Cook & Crisp tray, then place the tray in the bottom of the pot. Spray the tray with cooking spray.
2. Apply the mustard to the lamb ribs with a brush, and season with rosemary, salt, and pepper.
3. Close the lid and flip the SmartSwitch to AIR FRY/HOB. Select AIRFRY, set temperature to 180°C, and set time to 23 minutes (unit will need to preheat for 5 minutes, so set an external timer if desired). Press START/STOP to begin cooking.
4. When the unit is preheated and the time reaches 18 minutes, place the lamb ribs on the tray. Close the lid to begin cooking.
5. Meanwhile, mix the mint leaves and yogurt in a bowl.
6. Remove the lamb ribs to a plate and serve hot with the mint yogurt.

Japanese Tamari Pork

Prep Time: 6 minutes, Cook Time: 4 minutes, Serves: 4

INGREDIENTS:

- 450 g pork tenderloin, cut into 2.5 cm pieces
- 2 garlic cloves, crushed and chopped
- 30 ml cooking oil
- 2 tbsps. ginger, crushed and chopped
- 30 ml soy sauce
- 30 ml rice wine vinegar
- 25 g brown sugar
- 30 ml sake or dry sherry
- 15 ml white miso paste

DIRECTIONS:

1. Whisk together the miso and soy sauce in a small bowl. Keep aside.
2. Before getting started, be sure to remove the Cook & Crisp tray from the pot.
3. Flip the SmartSwitch to AIR FRY/HOB. Select SEAR/SAUTÉ and set to HI-5. Press START/STOP to begin cooking.
4. Heat the cooking oil in the pot until it shimmers.
5. Add the garlic, ginger, pork and sake and sauté for about 1 minute.
6. Place the brown sugar and rice wine vinegar and sauté for about 1 minute.
7. Stir in the miso and rice wine vinegar mixture and toss well.
8. Serve warm.

Chili Pork with Vegetable Quinoa

Prep: 15 minutes, Total Cook Time: 25-30 minutes, Steam: approx. 10-15 minutes, Cook: 15 minutes, Serves: 4

INGREDIENTS:

LEVEL 1 (BOTTOM OF POT)
- 330 g quinoa, rinsed
- 750 ml water
- 120 g spinach
- 1 bell pepper, chopped
- 3 stalks of celery, chopped
- ¼ tsp. salt

LEVEL 2 (TRAY)
- 4 pork chops
- 30 ml hot sauce
- 2 tbsps. cocoa powder
- 2 tsps. chilli powder
- ¼ tsp. ground cumin
- 1 tbsp. chopped parsley
- A pinch of salt and black pepper

DIRECTIONS:

1. Place all Level 1 ingredients in the pot and stir to combine.
2. Pull out the legs on the Cook & Crisp tray, then place the tray in the top position in the pot.
3. Stir all Level 2 ingredients in a large bowl and marinade for 5 minutes. Place the pork chops on top of the tray.
4. Close the lid and flip the SmartSwitch to RAPID COOKER.
5. Select SPEEDI MEALS, set temperature to 190°C, and set time to 15 minutes. Press START/STOP to begin cooking (the unit will steam for approx. 10 to 15 minutes, before countdown time begins).
6. When cooking is complete, remove the pork chops from the tray. Then use silicone-tipped tongs to grab the centre handle and remove the tray from the unit. Transfer the quinoa and vegetables to a bowl, then top with the pork chops. Serve warm.

Cheesy Sausage Balls and Bulgur Wheat

Prep: 10 minutes, Total Cook Time: 25 minutes, Steam: approx. 10 minutes, Cook: 15 minutes, Serves: 4

INGREDIENTS:

LEVEL 1 (BOTTOM OF POT)
- 190 g easy-cooked Bulgur wheat, rinsed
- 500 ml water
- 160 g fresh sweet potato, chopped

LEVEL 2 (TRAY)
- 340 g Lincolnshire sausages
- 170 g shredded Cheddar cheese
- 12 Cheddar cubes
- TOPPINGS:
- Mustard
- Pesto

DIRECTIONS:

1. Place all Level 1 ingredients in the pot and stir to combine.
2. Pull out the legs on the Cook & Crisp tray, then place the tray in the top position in the pot.
3. Mix the shredded cheese and sausage. Divide the mixture into 12 equal parts to be stuffed.
4. Add a cube of cheese to the centre of the sausage and roll into balls. Place the balls on top of the tray.
5. Close the lid and flip the SmartSwitch to RAPID COOKER.
6. Select SPEEDI MEALS, set temperature to 190°C, and set time to 15 minutes. Press START/STOP to begin cooking (the unit will steam for approx. 10 minutes, before countdown time begins).
7. When cooking is complete, remove the sausage balls from the tray. Then use silicone-tipped tongs to grab the centre handle and remove the tray from the unit. Transfer the Bulgur wheat and sweet potato to a bowl, then top with the sausage balls and desired toppings.

Cheddar Bacon Burst with Spinach

Prep Time: 5 minutes, Cook Time: 30 minutes, Serves: 8

INGREDIENTS:

- 30 rashers of bacon
- 1 tbsp. Chipotle seasoning
- 2 tsps. Italian seasoning
- 225 g Cheddar cheese
- 120 g raw spinach

DIRECTIONS:

1. Push in the legs on the Cook & Crisp tray, then place the tray in the bottom of the pot.
2. Weave the bacon into 15 vertical pieces and 12 horizontal pieces. Cut the extra 3 in half to fill in the rest, horizontally.
3. Season the bacon with Chipotle seasoning and Italian seasoning.
4. Add the cheese to the bacon.
5. Add the spinach and press down to compress.
6. Tightly roll up the woven bacon.
7. Line a baking sheet with kitchen foil and add plenty of salt to it.
8. Put the bacon on top of a cooling rack.
9. Close the lid and flip the SmartSwitch to AIR FRY/HOB. Select BAKE & ROAST, set temperature to 180°C, and set time to 35 minutes (unit will need to preheat for 5 minutes, so set an external timer if desired). Press START/STOP to begin cooking.
10. When the unit is preheated and the time reaches 30 minutes, place the rack with bacon on the tray. Close the lid to begin cooking.
11. Let cool for 15 minutes before slicing and serve.

Beef Meatballs and Tomato Meal

Prep: 15 minutes, Total Cook Time: 20-25 minutes, Steam: approx. 10-15 minutes, Cook: 10 minutes, Serves: 4

INGREDIENTS:

LEVEL 1 (BOTTOM OF POT)
- 150 g (or more) short grain brown rice, rinsed
- 35-50 g red, wild or black rice, rinsed
- 375 ml water
- ¼ tsp. sea salt

LEVEL 2 (TRAY)
- 450 g lean beef, minced
- 2 large eggs
- 30 g plain flour
- Salt and pepper, to taste
- 400 g diced tomatoes

DIRECTIONS:

1. Place all Level 1 ingredients in the pot and stir to combine.
2. Pull out the legs on the Cook & Crisp tray, then place the tray in the top position in the pot.
3. In a large bowl, thoroughly mix the beef, eggs, and flour, then sprinkle with salt and pepper. Mix well and make 6 meatballs of 4 cm. Place the meatballs on top of the tray. Top with the tomatoes.
4. Close the lid and flip the SmartSwitch to RAPID COOKER.
5. Select SPEEDI MEALS, set temperature to 180°C, and set time to 10 minutes. Press START/STOP to begin cooking (the unit will steam for approx. 10 to 15 minutes, before countdown time begins).
6. When cooking is complete, remove the meatballs and tomato from the tray. Then use silicone-tipped tongs to grab the centre handle and remove the tray from the unit. Transfer the rice to a bowl, then top with the meatballs and tomato.

Corned Beef

Prep Time: 15 minutes, Cook Time: 15 minutes, Serves: 4

INGREDIENTS:

- 1 (340-g) tin corned beef
- ¼ onion, chopped
- ¼ green bell pepper, chopped
- 60 ml water
- 10 ml tomato paste
- 5 ml vegetable oil
- ¼ tsp. dried thyme
- ¼ tsp. crushed red pepper flakes
- Salt and pepper to taste

DIRECTIONS:

1. Before getting started, be sure to remove the Cook & Crisp tray from the pot.
2. Flip the SmartSwitch to AIR FRY/HOB. Select SEAR/SAUTÉ and set to 3. Press START/STOP to begin cooking.
3. In the pot, heat the oil. Add the green pepper, onion, red pepper flakes and dried thyme and sauté for 7 minutes.
4. Set to LO-1 and toss in the tomato paste, salt and pepper. Simmer for 3 minutes.
5. Stir in the corned beef and water and simmer until all the liquid is absorbed. Serve warm.

Italian Lamb Chops with Avocado Mayo

Prep: 5 minutes, Total Cook Time: 24 minutes, Steam: approx. 4 minutes, Cook: 20 minutes, Serves: 2

INGREDIENTS:

- 125 ml water, for steaming
- 2 lamp chops
- 2 avocados
- 120 ml mayonnaise
- 15 ml lemon juice
- 2 tsps. Italian herbs

DIRECTIONS:

1. Pour 125 ml water into the pot. Push in the legs on the Cook & Crisp tray, then place the tray in the bottom position in the pot.
2. Sprinkle the lamb chops with the Italian herbs, then keep aside for 5 minutes.
3. Close the lid and flip the SmartSwitch to RAPID COOKER. Select STEAM AIR FRY, set temperature to 190°C, and set time to 20 minutes. Press START/STOP to begin cooking (the unit will steam for approx. 4 minutes, before countdown time begins).
4. Meanwhile, halve the avocados and open to remove the pits. Scoop the flesh into a blender. Add the mayonnaise and lemon juice and pulse until a smooth consistency is achieved.
5. Carefully transfer the chops to a plate and serve hot with the avocado mayo.

Spiced Lamb Steaks and Snap Pea Rice

Prep: 15 minutes, Total Cook Time: 25 minutes, Steam: approx. 10 minutes, Cook: 15 minutes, Serves: 3

INGREDIENTS:

LEVEL 1 (BOTTOM OF POT)
- 200 g easy-cooked brown rice, rinsed
- 200 g sugar snap peas
- 500 ml water
- Salt, to taste

LEVEL 2 (TRAY)
- ½ onion, roughly chopped
- 680 g boneless lamb sirloin steaks
- 5 garlic cloves, peeled
- 1 tbsp. fresh ginger, peeled
- 1 tsp. garam masala
- 1 tsp. ground fennel
- ½ tsp. ground cumin
- ½ tsp. ground cinnamon
- ½ tsp. cayenne pepper
- Salt and black pepper, to taste

TOPPINGS:
- Mint sauce
- Greek yogurt

DIRECTIONS:

1. Put the onion, garlic, ginger, and spices in a blender and pulse until smooth.
2. Coat the lamb steaks with this mixture on both sides and refrigerate to marinate for about 24 hours.
3. Place all Level 1 ingredients in the pot and stir to combine.
4. Pull out the legs on the Cook & Crisp tray, then place the tray in the top position in the pot.
5. Arrange the lamb steaks on top of the tray.
6. Close the lid and flip the SmartSwitch to RAPID COOKER.
7. Select SPEEDI MEALS, set temperature to 180°C, and set time to 15 minutes. Press START/STOP to begin cooking (the unit will steam for approx. 10 minutes, before countdown time begins).
8. When cooking is complete, remove the lamb steaks from the tray. Then use silicone-tipped tongs to grab the centre handle and remove the tray from the unit. Transfer the brown rice and snap peas to a bowl, then top with the lamb steaks and desired toppings.

Chinese Lamb

Prep Time: 15 minutes, Cook Time: 15 minutes, Serves: 4

INGREDIENTS:

- 450 g boneless leg of lamb, cut into 0.5-cm-thick slices
- 4 peeled fresh ginger slices, each about the size of a quarter
- 4 scallions, cut into 7.5-cm-long pieces, then thinly sliced lengthwise
- 3 garlic cloves, minced
- 2 whole dried red chili peppers (optional)
- 45 ml vegetable oil, divided
- 30 ml Shaoxing rice wine
- 15 ml dark soy sauce
- 6 g cornflour
- 5 ml sesame oil
- coarse salt

DIRECTIONS:

1. Stir together the dark soy, rice wine, garlic, cornflour and sesame oil in a large bowl. Place the lamb to the marinade and toss to coat well. Marinate for about 10 minutes.
2. Before getting started, be sure to remove the Cook & Crisp tray from the pot.
3. Flip the SmartSwitch to AIR FRY/HOB. Select SEAR/SAUTÉ and set to Hi-5. Press START/STOP to begin cooking.
4. Heat the pot until a drop of water sizzles and evaporates on contact.
5. Add 30 ml vegetable oil and swirl to coat the base of the pot well. Season the oil with the ginger, chilies (if using) and a pinch of salt. Let the aromatics sizzle in the oil for 30 seconds, swirling slowly.
6. Lift half the lamb from the marinade with tongs, shaking slightly to let the excess drip off. Reserve the marinade. Sear in the pot for about 2 to 3 minutes. Gently flip to sear on the other side for another 1 to 2 minutes. Sauté by tossing and flipping around in the pot immediately for 1 more minute. Transfer the lamb to a clean bowl. Pour in the remaining 15 ml vegetable oil and repeat this with the remaining lamb.
7. Take all of the lamb and the reserved marinade back to the pot and toss in the scallions. Sauté for another 1 minute, or until the lamb is cooked through and the marinade turns into a shiny sauce.
8. Transfer the lamb to a serving platter, discard the ginger and serve warm.

CHAPTER 5
POULTRY

Crispy Chicken Drumsticks

Prep: 5 minutes, Total Cook Time: 24 minutes, Steam: approx. 4 minutes, Cook: 20 minutes, Serves: 2

INGREDIENTS:

- 125 ml water, for steaming
- 2 tsps. paprika
- 1 tsp. packed brown sugar
- 1 tsp. garlic powder
- ½ tsp. dry mustard
- ½ tsp. salt
- Pinch pepper
- 4 (140-g) chicken drumsticks, trimmed
- 5 ml vegetable oil
- 1 scallion, green part only, sliced thin on bias

DIRECTIONS:

1. Pour 125 ml water into the pot. Pull out the legs on the Cook & Crisp tray, then place the tray in the top position in the pot.
2. Combine paprika, sugar, garlic powder, mustard, salt, and pepper in a bowl. Pat drumsticks dry with paper towels. Using metal skewer, poke 10 to 15 holes in skin of each drumstick. Rub with oil and sprinkle evenly with spice mixture. Arrange drumsticks on the tray, spaced evenly apart, alternating ends.
3. Close the lid and flip the SmartSwitch to RAPID COOKER. Select STEAM AIR FRY, set temperature to 210°C, and set time to 20 minutes. Press START/STOP to begin cooking (the unit will steam for approx. 4 minutes, before countdown time begins).
4. With 10 minutes remaining, open the lid and flip the drumsticks with tongs. Close the lid to continue cooking.
5. Transfer chicken to serving platter, tent loosely with aluminium foil, and let rest for 5 minutes. Sprinkle with scallion and serve.

Air Fried Chicken Tenders

Prep Time: 15 minutes, Cook Time: 18 minutes, Serves: 4

INGREDIENTS:

- cooking spray
- 340 g chicken breasts, cut into tenders
- 1 egg white
- 20 g plain flour
- 50 g panko bread crumbs
- Salt and black pepper, to taste

DIRECTIONS:

1. Push in the legs on the Cook & Crisp tray, then place the tray in the bottom of the pot. Spray the tray with cooking spray.
2. Season the chicken tenders with salt and black pepper.cone-tipped tongs to ensure even cooking. Close the lid to continue cooking.
3. When the time is up, serve chicken tenders hot.
4. Coat the chicken tenders with flour, then dip in egg whites and then dredge in the panko bread crumbs.
5. Close the lid and flip the SmartSwitch to AIR FRY/HOB. Select AIRFRY, set temperature to 190°C, and set time to 23 minutes (unit will need to preheat for 5 minutes, so set an external timer if desired). Press START/STOP to begin cooking.
6. When the unit is preheated and the time reaches 18 minutes, place the chicken tenders on the tray. Close the lid to begin cooking.
7. After 10 minutes, open the lid and toss the chicken tenders with sili

Cheesy Chicken Stuffed Mushrooms

Prep: 10 minutes, Total Cook Time: 19 minutes, Steam: approx. 4 minutes, Cook: 15 minutes, Makes: 12 mushrooms

INGREDIENTS:

- 125 ml water, for steaming
- 12 large fresh mushrooms, stems removed
- 225 g chicken meat, cubed
- 225 g imitation crabmeat, flaked
- 450 g butter
- Garlic powder, to taste
- 2 cloves garlic, peeled and minced
- Salt and black pepper, to taste
- 225 g cream cheese, softened
- Crushed red pepper, to taste

DIRECTIONS:

1. Pour 125 ml water into the pot. Push in the legs on the Cook & Crisp tray, then place the tray in the bottom position in the pot.
2. Heat butter on medium heat in a nonstick skillet and add chicken.
3. Sauté for about 5 minutes and stir in the remaining ingredients except mushrooms.
4. Stuff this filling mixture in the mushroom caps on the tray.
5. Close the lid and flip the SmartSwitch to RAPID COOKER. Select STEAM AIR FRY, set temperature to 190°C, and set time to 10 minutes. Press START/STOP to begin cooking (the unit will steam for approx. 4 minutes, before countdown time begins).
6. When cooking is complete, dish out to serve warm.

Chicken Meatballs

Prep: 10 minutes, Total Cook Time: 16 minutes, Steam: approx. 4 minutes, Cook: 12 minutes, Serves: 4

INGREDIENTS:

- 125 ml water, for steaming
- 450 g chicken, minced
- 2 garlic cloves, finely minced
- 1 tbsp. sweet Hungarian paprika
- 1 tsp. sugar
- 1 tsp. ground cumin
- 1 tsp. coarse salt
- ½ tsp. ground fennel
- ½ tsp. ground coriander
- ½ tsp. black pepper
- ½ tsp. cayenne pepper
- ¼ tsp. ground allspice

DIRECTIONS:

1. Pour 125 ml water into the pot. Push in the legs on the Cook & Crisp tray, then place the tray in the bottom position in the pot.
2. In a large bowl, carefully combine the chicken, garlic, paprika, salt, sugar, cumin, fennel, coriander, black pepper, cayenne, and allspice until all the ingredients are incorporated. Let sit for 30 minutes at room temperature, or cover and refrigerate for up to 24 hours.
3. Form the mixture into 16 meatballs. Arrange them in a single layer in the tray.
4. Close the lid and flip the SmartSwitch to RAPID COOKER. Select STEAM AIR FRY, set temperature to 180°C, and set time to 12 minutes. Press START/STOP to begin cooking (the unit will steam for approx. 4 minutes, before countdown time begins).
5. With 5 minutes remaining, open the lid and turn the meatballs over with tongs. Close the lid to continue cooking. Use a meat thermometer to ensure the meatballs have reached an internal temperature of 74°C.
6. Serve hot.

Chicken Manchurian

Prep: 10 minutes, Total Cook Time: 19 minutes, Steam: approx. 4 minutes, Cook: 15 minutes, Serves: 2

INGREDIENTS:

- 125 ml water, for steaming
- 450 g boneless, skinless chicken breasts, cut into 2.5 cm pieces
- 60 ml ketchup
- 1 tbsp. tomato-based chili sauce, such as Heinz
- 15 ml soy sauce
- 15 ml rice vinegar
- 10 ml vegetable oil
- 1 tsp. hot sauce, such as Tabasco
- ½ tsp. garlic powder
- ¼ tsp. cayenne pepper
- 2 scallions, thinly sliced
- Cooked white rice, for serving

DIRECTIONS:

1. Pour 125 ml water into the pot. Pull out the legs on the Cook & Crisp tray, then place the tray in the top position in the pot.
2. In a bowl, combine the chicken, ketchup, chili sauce, soy sauce, vinegar, oil, hot sauce, garlic powder, cayenne, and three-quarters of the scallions and toss until evenly coated.
3. Scrape the chicken and sauce into a metal cake pan and place the pan on the tray.
4. Close the lid and flip the SmartSwitch to RAPID COOKER. Select STEAM AIR FRY, set temperature to 190°C, and set time to 15 minutes. Press START/STOP to begin cooking (the unit will steam for approx. 4 minutes, before countdown time begins).
5. With 7 minutes remaining, open the lid and toss the chicken with tongs. Close the lid to continue cooking.
6. When cooking is complete, use tongs to remove the pan from the tray. Spoon the chicken and sauce over rice and top with the remaining scallions. Serve immediately.

Little Bay Yellow Curry

Prep Time: 15 minutes, Cook Time: 40 minutes, Serves: 4

INGREDIENTS:

- 30 ml vegetable oil
- 2½ tbsps. yellow curry powder
- 1 white onion, chopped
- 1 tsp. garlic salt
- 2 cloves garlic, crushed
- 1 (400 g) tin unsweetened coconut milk
- 450 g skinless, boneless chicken breast halves, chopped
- 80 ml chicken stock
- Salt and pepper to taste
- 1 small head cauliflower, chopped

DIRECTIONS:

1. Before getting started, be sure to remove the Cook & Crisp tray from the pot.
2. Flip the SmartSwitch to AIR FRY/HOB. Select SEAR/SAUTÉ and set to 3. Press START/STOP to begin cooking.
3. Heat the oil in the pot, sauté the onion and garlic until tender.
4. Stir in the chicken and sear for about 10 minutes.
5. Stir in the cauliflower, curry powder, garlic salt, coconut milk, chicken stock, salt and pepper.
6. Set to LO-1 and simmer for about 30 minutes, stirring occasionally.
7. Serve hot.

Cheesy Chicken Tacos

Prep: 10 minutes, Total Cook Time: 22 minutes, Steam: approx. 4 minutes, Cook: 18 minutes, Serves: 2 to 4

INGREDIENTS:

- 125 ml water, for steaming
- 1 tsp. chilli powder
- ½ tsp. ground cumin
- ½ tsp. garlic powder
- Salt and pepper, to taste
- Pinch cayenne pepper
- 450 g boneless, skinless chicken thighs, trimmed
- 5 ml vegetable oil
- 1 tomato, cored and chopped
- 2 tbsps. finely chopped red onion
- 2 tsps. minced red chilli
- 20 ml lime juice
- 6 to 12 (15-cm) corn tortillas, warmed
- 100 g shredded iceberg lettuce
- 85 g cheddar cheese, shredded

DIRECTIONS:

1. Pour 125 ml water into the pot. Pull out the legs on the Cook & Crisp tray, then place the tray in the top position in the pot.
2. Combine chilli powder, cumin, garlic powder, ½ tsp. salt, ¼ tsp. pepper, and cayenne in bowl. Pat chicken dry with paper towels, rub with oil, and sprinkle evenly with spice mixture. Place chicken on the tray.
3. Close the lid and flip the SmartSwitch to RAPID COOKER. Select STEAM AIR FRY, set temperature to 190°C, and set time to 18 minutes. Press START/STOP to begin cooking (the unit will steam for approx. 4 minutes, before countdown time begins).
4. With 8 minutes remaining, open the lid and flip the chicken with tongs. Close the lid to continue cooking.
5. Meanwhile, combine tomato, onion, red chilli, and lime juice in a bowl; season with salt and pepper to taste and set aside until ready to serve.
6. When cooking is complete, transfer chicken to a cutting board, let cool slightly, then shred into bite-size pieces using 2 forks. Serve chicken on warm tortillas, topped with salsa, lettuce, and cheddar.

Easy Tandoori Chicken

Prep: 5 minutes, Total Cook Time: 18 minutes, Serves: 4

INGREDIENTS:

- cooking spray
- 4 (140-g) low-sodium boneless, skinless chicken breasts
- 160 ml plain low-fat yogurt
- 2 garlic cloves, minced
- 30 ml freshly squeezed lemon juice
- 10 ml olive oil
- 2 tsps. curry powder
- ½ tsp. ground cinnamon

DIRECTIONS:

1. In a medium bowl, whisk the lemon juice, yogurt, curry powder, cinnamon, garlic, and olive oil.
2. Cut thin slashes into the chicken with a sharp knife. Place it to the yogurt mixture and turn to coat evenly. Allow to stand for about 10 minutes at room temperature.
3. Push in the legs on the Cook & Crisp tray, then place the tray in the bottom of the pot. Spray the tray with cooking spray.
4. Remove the chicken from the marinade and shake off any excess liquid. Discard any remaining marinade.
5. Close the lid and flip the SmartSwitch to AIR FRY/HOB. Select BAKE & ROAST, set temperature to 200°C, and set time to 23 minutes (unit will need to preheat for 5 minutes, so set an external timer if desired). Press START/STOP to begin cooking.
6. When the unit is preheated and the time reaches 18 minutes, place the chicken on the tray. Close the lid to begin cooking.
7. After 10 minutes, open the lid and turn the chicken pieces over with silicone-tipped tongs to ensure even cooking. Close the lid to continue cooking, until the chicken reaches an internal temperature of 74°C on a meat thermometer.
8. Serve hot.

Sausage Stuffed Chicken and Corn Rice

Prep: 10 minutes, Total Cook Time: 25 minutes, Steam: approx. 10 minutes, Cook: 15 minutes, Serves: 4

INGREDIENTS:

LEVEL 1 (BOTTOM OF POT)
- 200 g white rice, rinsed
- 200 g tinned corn kernels, drained
- 500 ml water or stock

LEVEL 2 (TRAY)
- 4 (110 g) skinless, boneless chicken breasts
- 4 sausages, casing removed
- 30 ml mustard sauce

TOPPINGS:
- Greek yogurt
- Guacamole

DIRECTIONS:

1. Place all Level 1 ingredients in the pot and stir to combine.
2. Pull out the legs on the Cook & Crisp tray, then place the tray in the top position in the pot.
3. Roll each chicken breast with a rolling pin for about 1 minute.
4. Arrange 1 sausage over each chicken breast and roll up.
5. Secure with toothpicks and transfer on top of the tray.
6. Close the lid and flip the SmartSwitch to RAPID COOKER.
7. Select SPEEDI MEALS, set temperature to 190°C, and set time to 15 minutes. Press START/STOP to begin cooking (the unit will steam for approx. 10 minutes, before countdown time begins).
8. When cooking is complete, remove the chicken from the tray. Then use silicone-tipped tongs to grab the centre handle and remove the tray from the unit. Transfer the rice and corn to a bowl, then top with the chicken and desired toppings.

Crisp Chicken and Creamy Polenta

Prep: 20 minutes, Total Cook Time: 25 minutes, Steam: approx. 10 minutes, Cook: 15 minutes, Serves: 4

INGREDIENTS:

LEVEL 1 (BOTTOM OF POT)
- 175 g polenta
- 375 ml water
- ½ tsp. sea salt
- 115 g cream cheese, at room temperature
- 60 ml milk
- ½ tsp. garlic powder
- ¼ tsp. porcini powder

LEVEL 2 (TRAY)
- 1 egg, beaten
- 50 g breadcrumbs
- 4 skinless, boneless chicken tenderloins
- 30 ml vegetable oil

TOPPINGS:
- toasted white sesame seeds
- 2 scallions, sliced thin

DIRECTIONS:

1. Place all Level 1 ingredients in the pot and stir to combine.
2. Pull out the legs on the Cook & Crisp tray, then place the tray in the top position in the pot.
3. Whisk the egg in a shallow dish and mix vegetable oil and breadcrumbs in another shallow dish.
4. Dip the chicken tenderloins in egg and then coat in the breadcrumb mixture.
5. Place the chicken tenderloins on top of the tray.
6. Close the lid and flip the SmartSwitch to RAPID COOKER.
7. Select SPEEDI MEALS, set temperature to 190°C, and set time to 15 minutes. Press START/STOP to begin cooking (the unit will steam for approx. 10 minutes, before countdown time begins).
8. When cooking is complete, remove the chicken tenderloins from the tray. Then use silicone-tipped tongs to grab the centre handle and remove the tray from the unit. Transfer the polenta to a bowl, then top with the chicken tenderloins and toppings. Serve hot.

Broccoli and Chicken

Prep Time: 15 minutes, Cook Time: 15 minutes, Serves: 4

INGREDIENTS:

- 15 ml Shaoxing rice wine
- 10 ml light soy sauce
- 1 tsp. minced garlic
- 1 tsp. cornflour
- ¼ tsp. sugar
- 340 g boneless, skinless chicken thighs, cut into 5 cm chunks
- 30 ml vegetable oil
- 4 peeled fresh ginger slices, about the size of a quarter
- coarse salt
- 450 g broccoli, cut into bite-size florets
- 30 ml water
- Red pepper flakes (optional)
- 60 ml store-bought black bean sauce

DIRECTIONS:

1. Before getting started, be sure to remove the Cook & Crisp tray from the pot.
2. In a small bowl, mix together the rice wine, light soy, garlic, cornflour, and sugar. Add the chicken and marinate for 10 minutes.
3. Flip the SmartSwitch to AIR FRY/HOB. Select SEAR/SAUTÉ and set to 4. Press START/STOP to begin cooking.
4. Pour in the vegetable oil in the pot. Add the ginger and a pinch of salt. Allow the ginger to sizzle for about 30 seconds, swirling gently.
5. Transfer the chicken to the pot, discarding the marinade. Sear the chicken for 4 to 5 minutes, until no longer pink. Add the broccoli, water, and a pinch of red pepper flakes (if using) and sear for 1 minute. Close the lid and cook the broccoli for 6 to 8 minutes, until it is crisp-tender.
6. Stir in the black bean sauce until coated and heated through, about 2 minutes, or until the sauce has thickened slightly and become glossy.
7. Discard the ginger, transfer to a platter, and serve hot.

Yummy Stuffed Chicken Breast with Fettuccine

Prep: 15 minutes, Total Cook Time: 25 minutes, Steam: approx. 10 minutes, Cook: 15 minutes, Serves: 4

INGREDIENTS:

LEVEL 1 (BOTTOM OF POT)
- 225 g fettuccine, broken in half
- 1 (400 g) tinned alfredo sauce
- 200 g fresh spinach leaves
- 500 ml water or stock

LEVEL 2 (TRAY)
- 2 (225 g) chicken fillets, skinless and boneless, each cut into 2 pieces
- 4 brie cheese slices
- 1 tbsp. chive, minced
- 4 cured ham slices
- Salt and black pepper, to taste

TOPPINGS:
- Hummus
- Tzatziki
- Fresh herbs

DIRECTIONS:

1. Place all Level 1 ingredients in the pot and stir to combine.
2. Pull out the legs on the Cook & Crisp tray, then place the tray in the top position in the pot.
3. Make a slit in each chicken piece horizontally and season with the salt and black pepper.
4. Insert cheese slice in the slits and sprinkle with chives.
5. Wrap each chicken piece with one ham slice and transfer on top of the tray.
6. Close the lid and flip the SmartSwitch to RAPID COOKER.
7. Select SPEEDI MEALS, set temperature to 200°C, and set time to 15 minutes. Press START/STOP to begin cooking (the unit will steam for approx. 10 minutes, before countdown time begins).
8. When cooking is complete, remove the chicken from the tray. Then use silicone-tipped tongs to grab the centre handle and remove the tray from the unit. Transfer the fettuccine and spinach to a bowl, then top with the chicken and desired toppings.

Curry Chicken with Dried Cranberry

Prep: 12 minutes, Total Cook Time: 19 minutes, Steam: approx. 4 minutes, Cook: 15 minutes, Serves: 4

INGREDIENTS:

- 125 ml water, for steaming
- cooking spray
- 10 ml olive oil
- 3 (140-g) low-sodium boneless, skinless chicken breasts, cut into 4 cm cubes
- 1 tart apple, chopped
- 55 g dried cranberries
- 120 ml low-sodium chicken broth
- 30 ml freshly squeezed orange juice
- 15 g cornflour
- 5 g curry powder
- Brown rice, cooked (optional)

DIRECTIONS:

1. Pour 125 ml water into the pot. Pull out the legs on the Cook & Crisp tray, then place the tray in the top position in the pot. Spray Multi-Purpose Tin or 20cm cake tin with cooking spray.
2. In a medium bowl, combine the chicken and olive oil. Scatter with the cornflour and curry powder. Toss to coat well. Stir in the apple and place to the tin. Then transfer the tin to the tray.
3. Close the lid and flip the SmartSwitch to RAPID COOKER. Select STEAM AIR FRY, set temperature to 190°C, and set time to 15 minutes. Press START/STOP to begin cooking (the unit will steam for approx. 4 minutes, before countdown time begins).
4. Open the lid and add the chicken broth, cranberries, and orange juice. Close the lid to continue cook for 10 minutes. Stir once during the cooking.
5. Serve over hot cooked brown rice, if desired.

Chicken Meatballs with Scallion

Prep: 10 minutes, Total Cook Time: 19 minutes, Steam: approx. 4 minutes, Cook: 15 minutes, Serves: 4

INGREDIENTS:

- 125 ml water, for steaming
- 450 g chicken, minced
- 2 scallions, finely chopped
- 40 g chopped fresh coriander leaves
- 20 g unsweetened desiccated coconut
- 15 ml hoisin sauce
- 15 ml soy sauce
- 10 ml sriracha or other hot sauce
- 5 ml toasted sesame oil
- ½ tsp. coarse salt
- 1 tsp. black pepper

DIRECTIONS:

1. Pour 125 ml water into the pot. Pull out the legs on the Cook & Crisp tray, then place the tray in the top position in the pot.
2. In a large bowl, gently mix the chicken, scallions, coriander, coconut, hoisin, soy sauce, sriracha, sesame oil, salt, and pepper until thoroughly combined (the mixture will be wet and sticky).
3. Place a sheet of parchment paper on the tray. Using a small scoop or teaspoon, drop rounds of the mixture in a single layer onto the parchment paper.
4. Close the lid and flip the SmartSwitch to RAPID COOKER. Select STEAM AIR FRY, set temperature to 180°C, and set time to 15 minutes. Press START/STOP to begin cooking (the unit will steam for approx. 4 minutes, before countdown time begins).
5. With 5 minutes remaining, open the lid and flip the meatballs with tongs. Close the lid to continue cooking.
6. When cooking is complete, transfer the meatballs to a serving platter. Serve hot.

Traditional Chicken Provençal

Prep Time: 16 minutes, Cook Time: 8 hours, Serves: 10

INGREDIENTS:

- 1.4 kg boneless, skinless chicken thighs
- 4 large tomatoes, seeded and chopped
- 3 bulbs fennel, cored and sliced
- 2 onions, chopped
- 2 red bell peppers, stemmed, seeded, and chopped
- 6 garlic cloves, minced
- 30 g sliced black Greek olives
- 4 sprigs fresh thyme
- 1 bay leaf
- 30 ml lemon juice

DIRECTIONS:

1. Before getting started, be sure to remove the Cook & Crisp tray.
2. Mix all the ingredients in the bottom of the pot.
3. Close the lid and flip the SmartSwitch to AIR FRY/HOB. Select SLOW COOK, set temperature to LOW, and set time to 8 hours. Press START/STOP to begin cooking, until the chicken registers 75ºC on a food thermometer.
4. Remove the thyme stems and bay leaf and discard.
5. Serve warm.

Chicken Pomegranate Stew

Prep Time: 15 minutes, Cook Time: 2 hours, Serves: 6

INGREDIENTS:

- 30 ml olive oil
- ½ tsp. cardamom (optional)
- 1 (225-g) chicken legs, cut up
- 25 g caster sugar (optional)
- 1 white onion, thinly sliced
- 225 g walnuts, toasted and finely ground in a food processor
- 1 tsp. salt
- 900 ml pomegranate juice

DIRECTIONS:

1. Before getting started, be sure to remove the Cook & Crisp tray from the pot.
2. Flip the SmartSwitch to AIR FRY/HOB. Select SEAR/SAUTÉ and set to 3. Press START/STOP to begin cooking.
3. Heat the olive oil in the pot. Sauté onions, and chicken for 20 minutes.
4. Add cardamom, walnut purée, pomegranate juice, and salt.
5. Heat until boiling. Set to LO-1 and cover the pot. Let everything simmer for 1½ hours.
6. Add some sugar. Simmer for 30 more minutes.
7. Serve and enjoy.

Chicken Tenders with Broccoli Quinoa Meal

Prep: 10 minutes, Total Cook Time: 25 minutes, Steam: approx. 10 minutes, Cook: 15 minutes, Serves: 4

INGREDIENTS:

LEVEL 1 (BOTTOM OF POT)
- 225 g quinoa, rinsed
- 150 g frozen peas
- 150 g frozen broccoli florets
- 1 tsp. herb seasoning
- 250 ml water or stock
- Salt and black pepper, to taste

LEVEL 2 (TRAY)
- 450 g chicken tenders
- 1 tsp. coarse salt
- 1 tsp. black pepper
- ½ tsp. smoked paprika
- 60 ml coarse mustard
- 30 ml honey
- 120 g finely crushed pecans

TOPPINGS:
- Salsa
- Sour cream

DIRECTIONS:

1. Place all Level 1 ingredients in the pot and stir to combine.
2. Pull out the legs on the Cook & Crisp tray, then place the tray in the top position in the pot.
3. Place the chicken in a large bowl. Sprinkle with the salt, pepper, and paprika. Toss until the chicken is coated with the spices. Add the mustard and honey and toss until the chicken is coated.
4. Put the pecans on a plate. Working with one piece of chicken at a time, roll the chicken in the pecans until both sides are coated. Lightly brush off any loose pecans. Place the chicken on top of the tray.
5. Close the lid and flip the SmartSwitch to RAPID COOKER.
6. Select SPEEDI MEALS, set temperature to 200°C, and set time to 15 minutes. Press START/STOP to begin cooking (the unit will steam for approx. 10 minutes, before countdown time begins).
7. When cooking is complete, remove the chicken from the tray. Then use silicone-tipped tongs to grab the centre handle and remove the tray from the unit. Transfer the quinoa and vegetables to a bowl, then top with the chicken and desired toppings.

CHAPTER 6
SNACK AND DESSERT

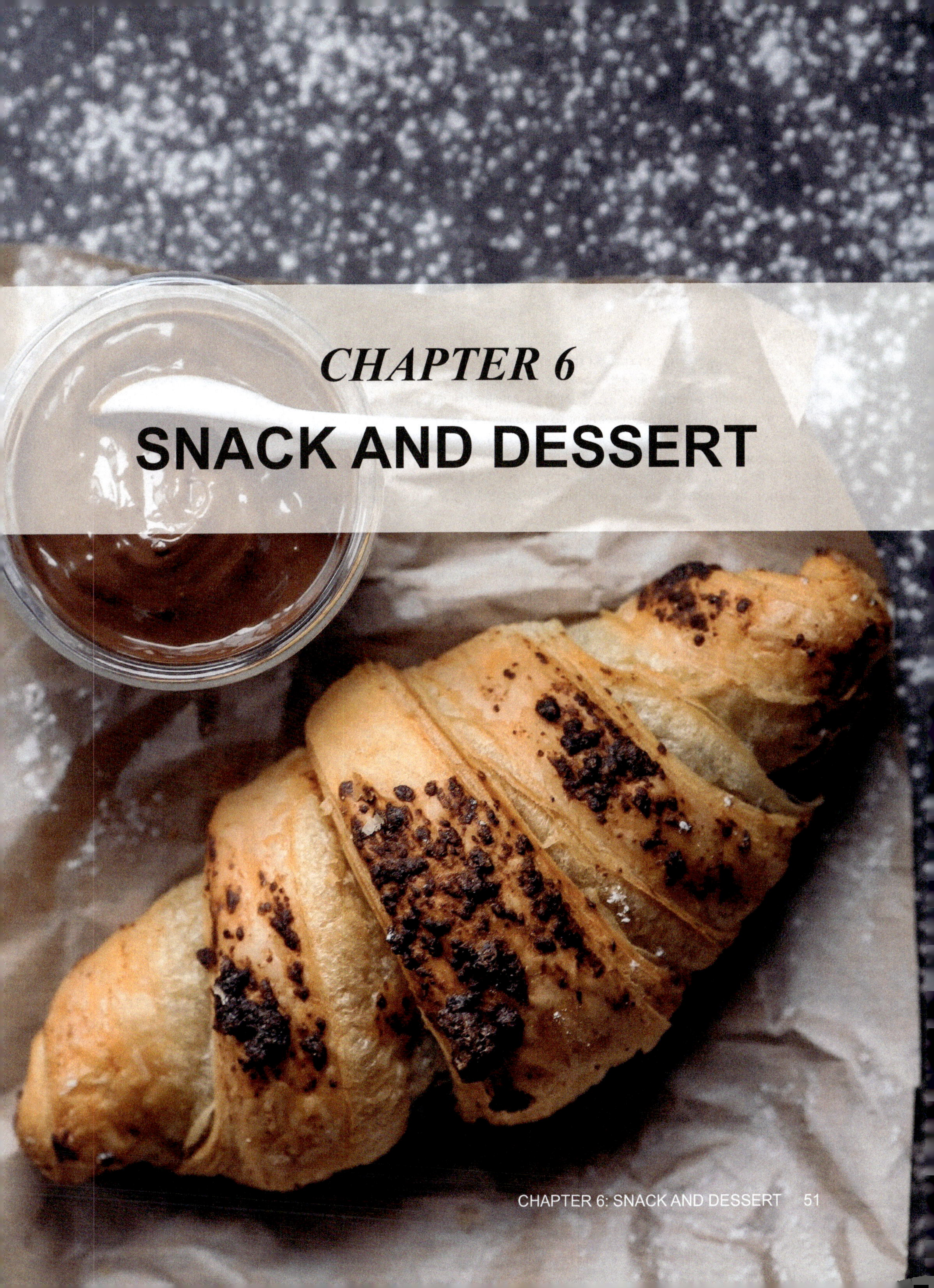

Spicy Kale Crisps

Prep Time: 5 minutes, Cook Time: 8 minutes, Serves: 4

INGREDIENTS:

- 150 g kale, large stems removed and chopped
- 10 ml rapeseed oil
- ¼ tsp. smoked paprika
- ¼ tsp. coarse salt
- Cooking spray

DIRECTIONS:

1. Push in the legs on the Cook & Crisp tray, then place the tray in the bottom of the pot. Spray the tray with cooking spray.
2. Close the lid and flip the SmartSwitch to AIR FRY/HOB. Select AIRFRY, set temperature to 150°C, and set time to 13 minutes (unit will need to preheat for 5 minutes, so set an external timer if desired). Press START/STOP to begin cooking.
3. In a large bowl, toss the kale, rapeseed oil, smoked paprika, and coarse salt.
4. When the unit is preheated and the time reaches 8 minutes, place the kale on the tray. Close the lid to begin cooking.
5. After 4 minutes, open the lid and toss the kale with silicone-tipped tongs to ensure even cooking. Close the lid to continue cooking, until crispy.
6. When cooking is complete, remove the kale and allow to cool on a wire rack for 3 to 5 minutes before serving.

Fluffy Orange Cake

Prep: 10 minutes, Total Cook Time: 37 minutes, Steam: approx. 20 minutes, Cook: 17 minutes, Serves: 8

INGREDIENTS:

- 500 ml water, for steaming
- Nonstick baking spray with flour
- 150 g plain flour
- 40 g yellow cornmeal
- 150 g caster sugar
- 1 tsp. bicarbonate of soda
- 60 ml safflower oil
- 300 ml orange juice, divided
- 1 tsp. vanilla
- 25 g icing sugar

DIRECTIONS:

1. Pour 500 ml water into the pot. Push in the legs on the Cook & Crisp tray, then place the tray in the bottom position in the pot. Spray Multi-Purpose Tin or 20cm cake tin with cooking spray.
2. In a medium bowl, combine the flour, cornmeal, caster sugar, bicarbonate of soda, safflower oil, 240 ml of the orange juice, and vanilla, and mix well.
3. Pour the batter into the tin and place on the tray.
4. Close the lid and flip the SmartSwitch to RAPID COOKER. Select STEAM BAKE, set temperature to 160°C, and set time to 17 minutes. Press START/STOP to begin cooking (the unit will steam for approx. 20 minutes, before countdown time begins).
5. When cooking is complete, transfer the cake on a cooling rack. Using a toothpick, make about 20 holes in the cake.
6. In a small bowl, combine remaining 60 ml of orange juice and the icing sugar and stir well. Drizzle this mixture over the hot cake slowly so the cake absorbs it.
7. Cool completely, then cut into wedges to serve.

Tasty Chicken Wings

Prep: 5 minutes, Total Cook Time: 22 minutes, Serves: 2 to 4

INGREDIENTS:

- cooking spray
- 570 g chicken wings, separated into flats and drumettes
- 15 g unsalted butter, melted
- 1 tsp. baking powder
- 1 tsp. cayenne pepper
- ¼ tsp. garlic powder
- coarse salt and freshly ground black pepper, to taste
- For serving:
- Blue cheese dressing
- Celery
- Carrot sticks

DIRECTIONS:

1. Push in the legs on the Cook & Crisp tray, then place the tray in the bottom of the pot. Spray the tray with cooking spray.
2. Put the chicken wings on a large plate, then sprinkle evenly with the cayenne, baking powder, and garlic powder. Toss the wings well with your hands, making sure the baking powder and seasonings evenly coat them, until evenly incorporated. Let the wings stand in the refrigerator for 1 hour or up to overnight.
3. Close the lid and flip the SmartSwitch to AIR FRY/HOB. Select AIRFRY, set temperature to 200°C, and set time to 27 minutes (unit will need to preheat for 5 minutes, so set an external timer if desired). Press START/STOP to begin cooking.
4. At the same time, season the wings with salt and black pepper.
5. When the unit is preheated and the time reaches 22 minutes, place the wings on the tray. Close the lid to begin cooking.
6. After 10 minutes, open the lid and toss the wings with silicone-tipped tongs to ensure even cooking. Close the lid to continue cooking.
7. When cooking is complete, transfer the wings to a bowl and toss with the butter while they're hot.
8. Place the wings on a platter and top with the blue cheese dressing, celery and carrot sticks.

Strawberries

Prep Time: 20 minutes, Cook Time: 7 hours, Serves: 6

INGREDIENTS:

- spray bottle of lemon juice
- 450 g strawberries, washed and hulled, then thin sliced

DIRECTIONS:

1. Lightly spray the strawberries with lemon juice. Spread on dehydrator rack.
2. Push in the legs on the Cook & Crisp tray, then place the tray in the bottom position in the pot. Put the rack with strawberries on the tray.
3. Close the lid and flip the SmartSwitch to AIR FRY/HOB. Select DEHYDRATE, set temperature to 60°C, and set time to 7 hours. Press START/STOP to begin cooking. When done, the strawberries should feel dry like paper and be somewhat flexible.
4. Remove the strawberries from the cooker, serve immediately ou vacuum seal in vacuum bags with an oxygen pack, and then double-bagged in Mylar bag.

Crispy Spiced Chickpeas

Prep: 10 minutes, Total Cook Time: 10 minutes, Serves: 4

INGREDIENTS:

- cooking spray
- 1 tin (425-g) chickpeas, rinsed and dried with paper towels
- 15 ml olive oil
- ½ tsp. dried chives
- ½ tsp. dried rosemary
- ½ tsp. dried parsley
- ¼ tsp. mustard powder
- ¼ tsp. cayenne pepper
- ¼ tsp. sweet paprika
- coarse salt and freshly ground black pepper, to taste

DIRECTIONS:

1. Push in the legs on the Cook & Crisp tray, then place the tray in the bottom of the pot. Spray the tray with cooking spray.
2. In a large bowl, mix all the ingredients, except for the coarse salt and black pepper, and toss until the chickpeas are well coated in the herbs and spices.
3. Close the lid and flip the SmartSwitch to AIR FRY/HOB. Select AIRFRY, set temperature to 180°C, and set time to 15 minutes (unit will need to preheat for 5 minutes, so set an external timer if desired). Press START/STOP to begin cooking.
4. When the unit is preheated and the time reaches 10 minutes, scrape the chickpeas and seasonings into the tray. Close the lid to begin cooking.
5. After 5 minutes, open the lid and toss the chickpeas with silicone-tipped tongs to ensure even cooking. Close the lid to continue cooking.
6. Take the crispy chickpeas to a bowl, season with coarse salt and black pepper, and serve hot.

Crispy Bacon-Wrapped Dates

Prep Time: 10 minutes, Cook Time: 7 minutes, Serves: 6

INGREDIENTS:

- 12 dates, pitted
- 6 rashers of high-quality bacon, cut in half
- Cooking spray

DIRECTIONS:

1. Push in the legs on the Cook & Crisp tray, then place the tray in the bottom of the pot. Spray the tray with cooking spray.
2. Wrap each date with half a rasher of bacon and secure with a toothpick.
3. Close the lid and flip the SmartSwitch to AIR FRY/HOB. Select AIRFRY, set temperature to 180°C, and set time to 12 minutes (unit will need to preheat for 5 minutes, so set an external timer if desired). Press START/STOP to begin cooking.
4. When the unit is preheated and the time reaches 7 minutes, place the bacon-wrapped dates on the tray. Close the lid to begin cooking, until the bacon is crispy.
5. When cooking is complete, remove the dates and allow to cool on a wire rack for 5 minutes before serving.

Raspberry Wontons

Prep Time: 15 minutes, Cook Time: 8 minutes, Serves: 12

INGREDIENTS:

For the Wonton Wrappers:
- cooking spray
- 500 g cream cheese, softened
- 1 Package of wonton wrappers
- 65 g icing sugar
- 1 tsp. vanilla extract

For the Raspberry Syrup:
- 340 g frozen raspberries
- 60 ml water
- 50 g sugar
- 1 tsp. vanilla extract

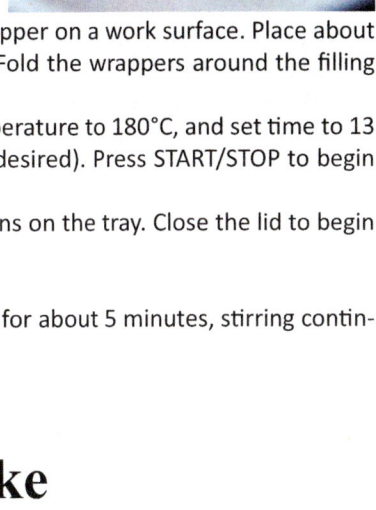

DIRECTIONS:

1. For the Wonton Wrappers:
2. Push in the legs on the Cook & Crisp tray, then place the tray in the bottom of the pot. Spray the tray with cooking spray.
3. Mix sugar, cream cheese and vanilla extract in a bowl and place a wonton wrapper on a work surface. Place about 1 tbsp. of the cream cheese mixture in the centre of each wonton wrapper. Fold the wrappers around the filling and seal the edges.
4. Close the lid and flip the SmartSwitch to AIR FRY/HOB. Select AIRFRY, set temperature to 180°C, and set time to 13 minutes (unit will need to preheat for 5 minutes, so set an external timer if desired). Press START/STOP to begin cooking.
5. When the unit is preheated and the time reaches 8 minutes, place the wontons on the tray. Close the lid to begin cooking.
6. For the Raspberry Syrup:
7. Put water, sugar, raspberries and vanilla in a skillet on medium heat and cook for about 5 minutes, stirring continuously.
8. Transfer the mixture into the food processor and blend until smooth.
9. Drizzle the raspberry syrup over the wontons to serve.

Walnut Chocolate Cake

Prep: 10 minutes, Total Cook Time: 50 minutes, Steam: approx. 20 minutes, Cook: 30 minutes, Serves: 4

INGREDIENTS:

- 750 ml water, for steaming
- Unsalted butter, at room temperature
- 3 large eggs
- 120 g almond flour
- 150 g sugar
- 80 ml double cream
- 25 g chopped walnuts
- 60 ml coconut oil, melted
- 25 g unsweetened cocoa powder
- 1 tsp. baking powder

DIRECTIONS:

1. Pour 750 ml water into the pot. Push in the legs on the Cook & Crisp tray, then place the tray in the bottom position in the pot. Generously butter Multi-Purpose Tin or 20cm cake tin. Line the bottom of the tin with parchment paper cut to fit.
2. In a large bowl, mix the eggs, almond flour, cream, sugar, coconut oil, cocoa powder, and baking powder. Beat with a hand mixer on medium speed until well blended and fluffy. Gently fold in the walnuts.
3. Pour the batter into the prepared tin and transfer the tin on the tray.
4. Close the lid and flip the SmartSwitch to RAPID COOKER. Select STEAM BAKE, set temperature to 200°C, and set time to 30 minutes. Press START/STOP to begin cooking (the unit will steam for approx. 20 minutes, before countdown time begins), until a knife (do not use a toothpick) inserted into the centre of the cake comes out clean.
5. Let the cake cool in the tin on a wire rack for 30 minutes before slicing and serving.

Frosting Cupcakes

Prep: 15 minutes, Total Cook Time: 32 minutes, Steam: approx. 20 minutes, Cook: 12 minutes, Serves: 12

INGREDIENTS:

- 250 ml water, for steaming
- cooking spray
- For the Cupcakes:
- 250 g refined flour
- 170 g peanut butter
- 3 eggs
- 90 g icing sugar
- 2 tsps. beetroot powder
- 1 tsp. cocoa powder
- For the Frosting:
- 225 g butter
- 225 g cream cheese
- 90 g icing sugar
- 60 ml strawberry sauce
- 1 tsp. vanilla essence

DIRECTIONS:

1. Pour 250 ml water into the pot. Push in the legs on the Cook & Crisp tray, then place the tray in the bottom position in the pot. Spray 12 silicon cups with cooking spray.
2. Mix all the Cupcakes ingredients in a large bowl until well combined.
3. Transfer the mixture into silicon cups and place on the tray.
4. Close the lid and flip the SmartSwitch to RAPID COOKER. Select STEAM BAKE, set temperature to 180°C, and set time to 12 minutes. Press START/STOP to begin cooking (the unit will steam for approx. 20 minutes, before countdown time begins).
5. Mix all the Frosting ingredients in a large bowl until well combined.
6. Top each cupcake evenly with frosting and serve.

Chocolate Cherry Turnovers

Prep: 10 minutes, Total Cook Time: 30 minutes, Steam: approx. 15 minutes, Cook: 15 minutes, Serves: 6

INGREDIENTS:

- 250 ml water, for steaming
- cooking spray
- 35 g milk or dark chocolate chips
- 30 ml thick, hot fudge sauce
- 20 g chopped dried cherries
- 1 (25-by-37-cm) sheet frozen puff pastry, thawed
- 1 egg white, beaten
- 25 g coconut sugar
- ½ tsp. cinnamon

DIRECTIONS:

1. Pour 250 ml water into the pot. Push in the legs on the Cook & Crisp tray, then place the tray in the bottom position in the pot. Spray the tray with cooking spray.
2. In a small bowl, combine the chocolate chips, fudge sauce, and dried cherries.
3. Roll out the puff pastry on a floured surface. Cut into 6 squares with a sharp knife.
4. Divide the chocolate chip mixture into the centre of each puff pastry square. Fold the squares in half to make triangles. Firmly press the edges with the tines of a fork to seal.
5. Brush the triangles on all sides sparingly with the beaten egg white. Sprinkle the tops with sugar and cinnamon. Transfer the triangles on the tray.
6. Close the lid and flip the SmartSwitch to RAPID COOKER. Select STEAM BAKE, set temperature to 180°C, and set time to 15 minutes. Press START/STOP to begin cooking (the unit will steam for approx. 15 minutes, before countdown time begins).
7. When cooking is complete, allow to cool for at least 20 minutes before serving.

Sweet and Spicy Carrot Sticks

Prep Time: 10 minutes, Cook Time: 12 minutes, Serves: 2

INGREDIENTS:

- cooking spray
- 1 large carrot, peeled and cut into sticks
- 1 tbsp. fresh rosemary, chopped finely
- 15 ml olive oil
- 8 g sugar
- ¼ tsp. cayenne pepper
- Salt and black pepper, to taste

DIRECTIONS:

1. Push in the legs on the Cook & Crisp tray, then place the tray in the bottom of the pot. Spray the tray with cooking spray.
2. Mix carrot with all other ingredients in a bowl until well combined.
3. Close the lid and flip the SmartSwitch to AIR FRY/HOB. Select AIRFRY, set temperature to 200°C, and set time to 17 minutes (unit will need to preheat for 5 minutes, so set an external timer if desired). Press START/STOP to begin cooking.
4. When the unit is preheated and the time reaches 12 minutes, place the carrot sticks on the tray. Close the lid to begin cooking.
5. After 6 minutes, open the lid and toss the carrot sticks with silicone-tipped tongs to ensure even cooking. Close the lid to continue cooking.
6. When cooking is complete, serve warm.

Potato and Bacon Nuggets

Prep Time: 5 minutes, Cook Time: 17 minutes, Serves: 4

INGREDIENTS:

- cooking spray
- 24 frozen potato nuggets
- 6 rashers of cooked bacon
- 30 ml maple syrup
- 100 g grated Cheddar cheese

DIRECTIONS:

1. Push in the legs on the Cook & Crisp tray, then place the tray in the bottom of the pot. Spray the tray with cooking spray.
2. Close the lid and flip the SmartSwitch to AIR FRY/HOB. Select AIRFRY, set temperature to 200°C, and set time to 22 minutes (unit will need to preheat for 5 minutes, so set an external timer if desired). Press START/STOP to begin cooking.
3. When the unit is preheated and the time reaches 17 minutes, place the potato nuggets on the tray. Close the lid to begin cooking. Meanwhile, cut the bacon into 2.5 cm pieces.
4. After 10 minutes, open the lid and flip the potato nuggets with silicone-tipped tongs to ensure even cooking. Top with the bacon and drizzle with the maple syrup. Close the lid to continue cooking.
5. With 2 minutes remaining, open the lid and top with the cheese. Close the lid to continue cooking, until the cheese is melted.
6. Serve hot.

Bacon Filled Poppers

Prep: 5 minutes, Total Cook Time: 22 minutes, Steam: approx. 4 minutes, Cook: 18 minutes, Serves: 4

INGREDIENTS:

- 125 ml water, for steaming
- 4 rashers of crispy cooked bacon
- 45 g butter
- 60 g jalapeno peppers, diced
- 70 g almond flour
- 30 g Cheddar cheese, white, shredded
- 1 pinch cayenne pepper
- 1 tbsp. bacon fat
- 1 tsp. coarse salt
- Black pepper, ground, to taste

DIRECTIONS:

1. Pour 125 ml water into the pot. Push in the legs on the Cook & Crisp tray, then place the tray in the bottom position in the pot.
2. Mix together butter with salt and water on medium heat in a skillet.
3. Whisk in the flour and sauté for about 3 minutes.
4. Dish out in a bowl and mix with the remaining ingredients to form a dough.
5. Wrap plastic wrap around the dough and refrigerate for about half an hour.
6. Make small popper balls out of this dough and arrange on the tray.
7. Close the lid and flip the SmartSwitch to RAPID COOKER. Select STEAM AIR FRY, set temperature to 200°C, and set time to 15 minutes. Press START/STOP to begin cooking (the unit will steam for approx. 4 minutes, before countdown time begins).
8. With 7 minutes remaining, open the lid and flip the balls with tongs. Close the lid to continue cooking.
9. When cooking is complete, dish out to serve warm.

Root Veggie Crisps with Herb Salt

Prep Time: 10 minutes, Cook Time: 10 minutes, Serves: 2

INGREDIENTS:

- 1 parsnip, washed
- 1 small beetroot, washed
- 1 small turnip, washed
- ½ small sweet potato, washed
- 5 ml olive oil
- Cooking spray

For the Herb Salt:
- ¼ tsp. coarse salt
- 2 tsps. finely chopped fresh parsley

DIRECTIONS:

1. Push in the legs on the Cook & Crisp tray, then place the tray in the bottom of the pot. Spray the tray with cooking spray.
2. Peel and thinly slice the parsnip, beetroot, turnip, and sweet potato, then place the vegetables in a large bowl, add the olive oil, and toss.
3. Close the lid and flip the SmartSwitch to AIR FRY/HOB. Select AIRFRY, set temperature to 200°C, and set time to 15 minutes (unit will need to preheat for 5 minutes, so set an external timer if desired). Press START/STOP to begin cooking.
4. When the unit is preheated and the time reaches 10 minutes, place the vegetables on the tray. Close the lid to begin cooking.
5. After 5 minutes, open the lid and toss the vegetables with silicone-tipped tongs to ensure even cooking. Close the lid to continue cooking.
6. When cooking is complete, remove the chips to a serving plate, then sprinkle the herb salt on top and allow to cool for 2 to 3 minutes before serving.

Tropical Fruit Sticks

Prep Time: 5 minutes, Cook Time: 10 minutes, Serves: 4

INGREDIENTS:
- cooking spray
- ½ fresh pineapple, cut into sticks
- 25 g desiccated coconut

DIRECTIONS:
1. Push in the legs on the Cook & Crisp tray, then place the tray in the bottom of the pot. Spray the tray with cooking spray.
2. Coat the pineapple sticks in the desiccated coconut.
3. Close the lid and flip the SmartSwitch to AIR FRY/HOB. Select AIRFRY, set temperature to 180°C, and set time to 15 minutes (unit will need to preheat for 5 minutes, so set an external timer if desired). Press START/STOP to begin cooking.
4. When the unit is preheated and the time reaches 10 minutes, place the pineapple sticks on the tray. Close the lid to begin cooking.
5. After 5 minutes, open the lid and flip the pineapple sticks with silicone-tipped tongs to ensure even cooking. Close the lid to continue cooking.
6. When cooking is complete, serve immediately.

Fruity Crumble

Prep Time: 15 minutes, Cook Time: 20 minutes, Serves: 4

INGREDIENTS:
- cooking spray
- 225 g fresh apricots, pitted and cubed
- 150 g fresh blackberries
- 110 g plain flour
- 15 ml cold water
- 55 g chilled butter, cubed
- 80 g caster sugar, divided
- 15 ml fresh lemon juice
- Pinch of salt

DIRECTIONS:
1. Push in the legs on the Cook & Crisp tray, then place the tray in the bottom of the pot. Spray Multi-Purpose Tin or 20cm cake tin with cooking spray.
2. Mix apricots, blackberries, 25 g sugar and lemon juice in a bowl.
3. Combine the remaining ingredients in a bowl and mix until a crumbly mixture is formed.
4. Pour the apricot mixture in the tin and top with the crumbly mixture.
5. Close the lid and flip the SmartSwitch to AIR FRY/HOB. Select BAKE & ROAST, set temperature to 200°C, and set time to 25 minutes (unit will need to preheat for 5 minutes, so set an external timer if desired). Press START/STOP to begin cooking.
6. When the unit is preheated and the time reaches 20 minutes, place the tin on the tray. Close the lid to begin cooking.
7. Dish out in a bowl and serve warm.

Doughnuts Pudding

Prep Time: 15 minutes, Cook Time: 50 minutes, Serves: 4

INGREDIENTS:

- cooking spray
- 6 glazed doughnuts, cut into small pieces
- 130 g frozen sweet cherries
- 75 g sultanas
- 90 g semi-sweet chocolate baking chips
- 4 egg yolks
- 50 g caster sugar
- 1 tsp. ground cinnamon
- 360 ml whipping cream

DIRECTIONS:

1. Push in the legs on the Cook & Crisp tray, then place the tray in the bottom of the pot. Spray Multi-Purpose Tin or 20cm cake tin with cooking spray.
2. Mix doughnut pieces, cherries, sultanas, chocolate chips, sugar, and cinnamon in a large bowl.
3. Whisk the egg yolks with whipping cream in another bowl until well combined.
4. Combine the egg yolk mixture into the doughnut mixture and mix well.
5. Arrange the doughnuts mixture evenly into the tin.
6. Close the lid and flip the SmartSwitch to AIR FRY/HOB. Select BAKE & ROAST, set temperature to 160°C, and set time to 55 minutes (unit will need to preheat for 5 minutes, so set an external timer if desired). Press START/STOP to begin cooking.
7. When the unit is preheated and the time reaches 50 minutes, place the tin on the tray. Close the lid to begin cooking.
8. Serve warm.

APPENDIX 1: NINJA SPEEDI TIMETABLE

Steam Air Fry Chart

INGREDIENT	AMOUNT	PREPARATION	WATER	ORIENTATION	TEMP	COOK TIME
POULTRY						
Chicken breasts	2 (175g each)	None	125ml	Top	190°C	15-20 mins
Chicken breasts, breaded	4 (175g each)	None	125ml	Top	190°C	18-20 mins
Chicken drumsticks	1kg	None	125ml	Top	210°C	25-30 mins
Chicken thighs (bone in)	1kg	None	125ml	Top	190°C	20-25 mins
Chicken thighs (boneless)	4 (100-125g each)	None	125ml	Top	190°C	15-18 mins
Chicken wings	500g	None	125ml	Bottom	220°C	15 mins
Whole chicken	2-2.5kg	Trussed	250ml	Bottom	180°C	60-80 mins
Turkey breast	1.4-2.4kg	None	250ml	Bottom	180°C	45-55 mins
BEEF						
Topside	1.5kg	None	250ml	Bottom	180°C	45 mins for medium rare
Rolled rib	1.5kg	None	250ml	Bottom	180°C	30-32 mins for medium rare
PORK						
Pork chops	4 thick-cut, bone-in (250g each)	Bone in	125ml	Top	190°C	25-30 mins
Pork chops	4 boneless (100-125g each)	Boneless	125ml	Top	190°C	20-25 mins
Pork loin	1kg	None	250ml	Bottom	180°C	35-40 mins
LAMB						
Leg of lamb	1.5kg	None	250ml	Bottom	180°C	37-40 mins
FISH						
Cod	4 (150g each)	None	125ml	Top	220°C	9-12 mins
Salmon	4 (150g each)	None	65ml	Top	220°C	7-10 mins

*NOTE: Crisper tray position varies, as specified in chart. Steam will take approximately 4-10 minutes to build.

Steam Air Fry Chart

INGREDIENT	AMOUNT	PREPARATION	WATER	ORIENTATION	TEMP	COOK TIME
FROZEN POULTRY						
Chicken breasts	4 (175g each)	None	250ml	Top	200°C	15-20 mins
Chicken drumsticks	1kg	None	125ml	Top	180°C	20-25 mins
Chicken thighs	1kg	None	125ml	Top	200°C	20-22 mins
Chicken wings	500g	None	125ml	Bottom	220°C	15 mins
FROZEN BEEF						
Steak, sirloin	2 (225g each)	None	250ml	Top	180°C	12-18 mins
FROZEN FISH						
Salmon	4 (120g each)	None	65ml	Top	220°C	7-10 mins
Cod	4 (120g each)	None	125ml	Top	220°C	10-15 mins
FROZEN PORK						
Pork chops with bone	2 (250g each)	None	125ml	Bottom	190°C	23-28 mins
Sausages	450g	None	125ml	Bottom	190°C	10-12 mins
VEGETABLES						
Beetroot	1kg	Peel, cut into 1.25cm cubes	125ml	Bottom	200°C	30-35 mins
Broccoli	400g	Whole, remove stem	125ml	Bottom	210°C	15-20 mins
Brussels sprouts	1kg	Cut in half, trim ends	125ml	Bottom	220°C	10-12 mins
Butternut squash	1kg	Cut in half, deseed	125ml	Bottom	190°C	22-25 mins
Carrots	1kg	Peel, cut into 1.25cm rounds	125ml	Bottom	200°C	22-28 mins
Parsnip	500g	Cut into 2.5cm pieces	125ml	Bottom	200°C	30-35 mins
Potatoes, King Edward/Maris Piper/Russet	1kg	Cut into 2.5cm wedges	125ml	Bottom	220°C	30-35 mins
	4, 800g	Whole	125ml	Bottom	200°C	25-30 mins
Sweet potatoes	1kg	Cut into 2.5cm cubes	125ml	Bottom	200°C	20 mins

*NOTE: Crisper tray position varies, as specified in chart. Steam will take approximately 4-10 minutes to build.

Air Fry Chart for the Crisper Tray, bottom position

INGREDIENT	AMOUNT	PREPARATION	OIL	TEMP	COOK TIME
VEGETABLES					
Asparagus	250g	Trim stems	2 tsp	200°C	7-8 mins
Bell peppers	4 (750g)	Whole	None	200°C	20 mins
Cauliflower	400g	Cut in 2.5-5cm florets	1 tbsp	200°C	12-14 mins
Corn on the cob	4 ears (1kg)	Whole ears, husk removed	1 tbsp	200°C	12-15 mins
Courgette	500g	Cut in quarters lengthwise, then into 2.5cm pieces	1 tbsp	200°C	11-12 mins
Green beans	350g	Trimmed	1 tbsp	200°C	7-10 mins
Kale for chips	400g	Torn in pieces, stems removed	None	150°C	8-12 mins
Mushrooms	300g	Wipe, quarter	1 tbsp	200°C	7-8 mins
Potatoes, King Edward/Maris Piper/Russets	500g	Hand cut chips, thin	½-3 tbsp	200°C	18-22 mins
Potatoes, King Edward/Maris Piper/Russets	500g	Hand cut chips, thick	½-3 tbsp	200°C	20-22 mins
Potatoes, sweet	1kg	Cut into 2.5cm cubes	1 tbsp	200°C	14-16 mins
BEEF					
Burgers	4 (125g each)	1.5-1.75cm thick	None	190°C	10 mins
Steak	2 (225g each)	None	Brushed with oil	200°C	8-12 mins
PORK					
Bacon	6 rashers, (200g)	Lay rashers evenly over tray	None	170°C	10 mins
Gammon steak	1 (225g)	Whole	None	200°C	10-12 mins
Sausages	8 (450g)	None	None	200°C	7-8 mins

*****TIP** When using Air Fry, add 5 minutes to the suggested cook time for the unit to preheat before you add ingredients.

Air Fry Chart for the Crisper Tray, bottom position

INGREDIENT	AMOUNT	PREPARATION	OIL	TEMP	COOK TIME
FROZEN FOODS					
Chicken nuggets	380g	None	None	200°C	10 mins
Fish fillets (battered)	440g	None	None	200°C	14 mins
Fish fingers	10 (280g)	None	None	200°C	9-10 mins
Hash browns	8 (360g)	None	None	200°C	14 mins
Roast potatoes	700g	None	None	200°C	25-30 mins
Mozzarella sticks	360g	None	None	200°C	6-7 mins
Onion rings	300g	None	None	200°C	10-12 mins
Scampi	9 jumbo pieces (230g)	None	None	200°C	7 mins
Sweet potato fries	500g	None	None	200°C	15 mins
Veggie burgers	4 (350g)	None	None	190°C	14 mins
Veggie sausages	6 (270g)	None	None	200°C	7-8 mins
FROZEN CHIPS					
Light straight chips	500g	None	None	200°C	14 mins
Chunky chips	500g	None	None	200°C	17 mins
Crinkle cut chips	500g	None	None	200°C	16 mins
French fries	500g	None	None	180°C	14 mins
Gastro chips	700g	None	None	200°C	18-20 mins
Potato wedges	650g	None	None	200°C	15 mins
Skin-on chips	500g	None	None	200°C	16-17 mins
FISH & SEAFOOD					
Fishcakes	2 (150g each)	None	None	200°C	8-10 mins
Prawns	16 jumbo	Raw, whole, tails on	1 tbsp	200°C	7-10 mins

*TIP When using Air Fry, add 5 minutes to the suggested cook time for the unit to preheat before you add ingredients.

Steam Chart for the Crisper Tray, bottom position

INGREDIENT	AMOUNT	PREPARATION	LIQUID	COOK TIME
VEGETABLES				
Asparagus	250g	Whole spears	250ml	5-7 mins
Broccoli	300g	Cut into 2.5-5cm florets	250ml	5-9 mins
Brussels sprouts	400g	Whole, trimmed	250ml	10-15 mins
Butternut squash	500g	Peeled, cut into 2.5cm cubes	250ml	10-15 mins
Carrots	500g	Peeled, cut into 2.5cm pieces	250ml	10-15 mins
Cauliflower	400g	Peeled, cut into 2.5-5cm florets	250ml	5-10 mins
Corn on the cob	4 ears	Whole, husks removed	250ml	8-10 mins
Green beans	200g	Whole, trimmed	250ml	8-12 mins
Potatoes	500g	Peeled, cut into 2.5cm pieces	325ml	12-17 mins
Potatoes, baby new	500g	Whole pieces	325ml	15-20 mins
Sweet potatoes	500g	Cut into 1.25cm cubes	250ml	8-14 mins

Dehydrate Chart for the Crisper Tray, bottom position

INGREDIENT	PREPARATION	TEMP	DEHYDRATE TIME
FRUITS & VEGETABLES			
Apple chips	Cut into 3mm slices, remove core, rinse in lemon water, pat dry	60°C	7-8 hrs
Bananas	Peel, cut into 3mm slices	60°C	8-10 hrs
Fresh herbs	Rinse, pat dry, remove stems	60°C	4-6 hrs
Ginger root	Cut into 3mm slices	60°C	6 hrs
Mangoes	Peel, cut into 3mm slices, remove stone	60°C	6-8 hrs
Mushrooms	Clean with soft brush or wipe with damp kitchen paper	60°C	6-8 hrs
Pineapple	Peel, cut into 3mm-1.25cm slices, core removed	60°C	6-8 hrs
Strawberries	Cut in half or into 1.25cm slices	60°C	6-8 hrs
Tomatoes	Cut into 3mm slices; steam if planning to rehydrate	60°C	6-8 hrs
MEAT, POULTRY, FISH			
Beef, chicken, salmon jerky	Cut into 6mm slices, marinate overnight	70°C	5-7 hrs

*TIP Most fruits and vegetables take between 6 and 8 hours (at 60°C) to dehydrate; meats take between 5 and 7 hours (at 70°C). The longer you dehydrate your ingredients, the crispier they will be.

APPENDIX 2: RECIPES INDEX

A

ACORN SQUASH
Curried Winter Squash 28
APPLE
Cinnamon Apple Nut Muffins 4
APRICOT
Fruity Crumble 59
AUBERGINE
Italian Aubergine Slices 22

B

BACON
Cheddar Bacon Burst with Spinach 36
Potato and Bacon Nuggets 27
BEEF
Beef Meatballs and Tomato Meal 37
Gourmet Meatloaf 32
BEEF EYE OF ROUND
Sweet and Spicy Pepper Beef Jerky 32
BEEF ROAST
Tasty Beef Roast 33
BRUSSELS SPROUTS
Brussels Sprouts 26
BUTTON MUSHROOM
Delish Mushroom Frittata 10

C

CANNELLINI BEAN
Rosemary White Beans with Onion 29
CARROT
Sweet and Spicy Carrot Sticks 57
CATFISH
Spiced Catfish with Spaghetti 17
CHERRY
Doughnuts Pudding 60
CHICKEN
Broccoli and Chicken Quiche 5
Cheesy Chicken Stuffed Mushrooms 42
Chicken Meatballs 42
Chicken Meatballs with Scallion 48
CHICKEN BREAST
Sausage Stuffed Chicken and Corn Rice 46
Air Fried Chicken Tenders 41
Easy Tandoori Chicken 45
Curry Chicken with Dried Cranberry 48
Chicken Manchurian 43
Little Bay Yellow Curry 43
CHICKEN DRUMSTICK
Crispy Chicken Drumsticks 41
CHICKEN FILLET
Yummy Stuffed Chicken Breast with Fettuccine 47
CHICKEN LEG
Chicken Pomegranate Stew 49
CHICKEN TENDER
Chicken Tenders with Broccoli Quinoa Meal 50
CHICKEN TENDERLOIN
Crisp Chicken and Creamy Polenta 46
CHICKEN THIGH
Broccoli and Chicken 47
Cheesy Chicken Tacos 44
Traditional Chicken Provençal 49
CHICKEN WING
Tasty Chicken Wings 53
CHICKPEA
Crispy Spiced Chickpeas 54
CHOCOLATE CHIP
Chocolate Cherry Turnovers 56
CHUCK SHOULDER ROAST
Beef Roast with Mushroom and Carrot 33
COD
Tasty Cod Sticks 13
Mediterranean Cod and Veggies 16
CORNED BEEF
Corned Beef 37
COURGETTE
Vegetable Ratatouille 26

D-G

DATE

Crispy Bacon-Wrapped Dates 54
GREEN BEAN
French Green Beans with Shallot 25

H-K

HAM
Ham and Egg Toast Cups 8
JALAPENO PEPPER
Bacon Filled Poppers 58
KALE
Spicy Kale Crisps 52
KING PRAWN
Spicy Orange Prawn 17

L

LAMB LEG
Chinese Lamb 39
Roasted Lamb Leg 34
LAMB RIB
Mustard Lamb Ribs 34
LAMB SIRLOIN STEAK
Spiced Lamb Steaks and Snap Pea Rice 38
LAMP CHOP
Italian Lamb Chops with Avocado Mayo 38

O

OKRA
Crispy Cornmeal Okra 23

P

PARSNIP
Honey-Glazed Parsnips, Carrots and Fennel 28
Root Veggie Crisps with Herb Salt 58
PEPPERONI
Pitta Pepperoni Pizza 3
Mozzarella Pitta Pizza 7
PINEAPPLE
Tropical Fruit Sticks 59

PORK CHOP
Chili Pork with Vegetable Quinoa 35
PORK LOIN ROAST
Citrus Roasted Pork 31
PORK TENDERLOIN
Japanese Tamari Pork 35
Classic Sweet and Sour Pork and Pineapple 31
POTATO
Sweetcorn Sausage Frittata 4
Kale and Potato Nuggets 6
Garlic Root Vegetable Hash 27
Roasted Potatoes and Asparagus 25
PRAWN
Creamy Breaded Prawn 12
Bacon-Wrapped Prawn 14
Prawn and Polenta with Tomato 19

R

RASPBERRY
Raspberry Wontons 55
RED CABBAGE
Braised Sweet and Sour Red Cabbage 24

S

SALMON
Tasty Ricotta Toasts 6
Panko Salmon Patties 14
Salmon and Veggies Ratatouille 16
Easy Roasted Salmon 15
Salmon Vegetables Chowder 18
Honey Glazed Salmon with Sweet Potato Rice 20
SAUSAGE
Quick Sausage Pizza 9
Cheesy Sausage Balls and Bulgur Wheat 36
SCALLOP
Garlic Scallops 12
Scallops with Capers Sauce 15
Rice Noodles with Broccoli and Scallop 19
SHISHITO PEPPER
Blistered Shishito Peppers 24
SPINACH
Spinach and Egg Cups 3

Healthy Egg Veggie Frittata	8
STRAWBERRY	
Strawberries	53
SWEET POTATO	
Sweet Potato Chips	22
Sweet Potatoes with Carrot	27
SWEETCORN	
Buttered Sweetcorn on the Cob	29

T

TOFU	
Tofu Scramble Omelette	10
TOMATO	
Ham and Tomato Omelette	7
Mini Tomato and Gouda Quiche	9
Cheese Stuffed Tomatoes	23
TUNA	
Tuna Patty Sliders	13
Savory Tuna Cakes	18

W

WALNUT	
Walnut Chocolate Cake	55

Printed in Great Britain
by Amazon